Jesus
And
Untouchability

M.R. ARULRAJA

CHERRY BOOKS

Ewing, NJ 08638, USA

ISBN: 0692826378
ISBN-13: 978-0692826379

Dedicated to Kaniappa Aiyya

Past president of Mangudi village, who led his people to freedom, fearlessly fighting the oppressing communities around, as a true accomplished marshal artist, often risking his life.

May his soul rest in peace.

Jesus And Untouchability

CONTENTS

ACKNOWLEDGEMENTS

This book has been made possible by the help of many people. The Dalit parishioners of Ongur and Mallikapuram along with their parish priests – Fr Mark Stephen SJ and Fr Jerry Rosario SJ – gave me shelter and facilitated the process of my learning theology. The Dalit youth in Andhra Pradesh and Tamil Nadu accompanied me in searching the gospels. I thank them all for all that they shared with me.

I offer my sincere thanks to my professors Fr. A. M. Lourdusamy SJ, Fr. S. Arockiasamy SJ, and Fr. George Koonthanam who helped me to look at Jesus in a very new perspective in the company of the oppressed people. Fr Francis Jayapathy SJ taught me the anthropological perspectives of celebrations and myths that greatly helped my study of religion.

I express my deep sentiments of gratitude to Fr. A.X.J Bosco SJ, who has rendered the foreword.

Quite a few of my friends who helped me greatly with the writing of this book prefer to be anonymous. I thank them also. I gratefully acknowledge the editorial assistance offered by Fr. Poornam de Mel, Mr. D. Gopi, Mr. Antony Arulraj and Mr. Nair. A very special word of thanks to Mr. Antony Xavier and Joseph Poonolly for their personal interest in encouraging me to complete this book, which is a revised version of my earlier book Jesus the Dalit, and for their further support in editing and publishing this book.

Thanks to Nirmala my wife, and Poornima my daughter for their support while writing the book.

The Biblical Quotes in this book are from New Revised Standard Version (NRSV) under their general licensing terms.

M. R. Arulraja

Jesus And Untouchability

FOREWORD

The Church is divine and human. The Church grows mature and evolves to be more Christian day by day. We often do not see things clearly; we are afraid to see because it will hurt us. Sometimes, we do not want to see because we feel comfortable to be where we are. And so, as the leaders of the Church and as good Christians, we must humbly accept our ignorance and sinfulness. We must open our eyes and see; we must make sincere efforts to follow the great commandment of love in every practical aspect of life.

This book, if read with an open mind, will enlighten us as to how we are caught up in a terrible trap of a discriminatory system which, to say the least, denies human dignity and distorts the image of God within us. It dehumanizes both the oppressor and the oppressed. Having an honest and critical look at ourselves, keeping off our defenses and rationalizations, will show us innumerable possibilities of confronting the evils of this discriminatory system, with Christian values.

I appreciate Mr. Arulraja's openness, honesty and courage to critically look at the reality of our society and the Church and speak out boldly. The scriptural analysis and interpretations will go a long way to throw light on the present situation so that we do not become victims of evil, but put up a brave fight to gain the freedom of the children of God.

FR. A.X.J. BOSCO SJ

Former Regional President,
Conference of Religious Congregations;
Former Jesuit Provincial Superior,
Andhra Pradesh, South India.

INTRODUCTION

The struggle of Jesus was precisely against the practice of untouchability prevalent in his place and time. Jesus was not exactly giving an example for the oppressed to carry their cross meekly unto death. He was rather asking them to fight discrimination even if it would cost them their lives! His struggle should become directly relevant to them. They should discover in Jesus their hero, their leader, their God who died for their liberation.

The New Testament also speaks of the struggle of his apostles to keep themselves faithful to the Way he carved out for them. Paul emerges as the valiant champion of the cause of the untouchables as he affirms the equality of all in Jesus. When Peter discriminated against non-Jewish Christians of Antioch on the question of table fellowship, Paul, condemned him. For Paul, such a practice of discrimination went against the truth of the gospels.

We find in the Bible that untouchability as a practice of discrimination existed in Israel at the time of Jesus and that it had its roots in the Bible itself!

This book also examines the way the Good News was compromised with the system of discrimination down the centuries, and the anomaly it created to the Christian values of brotherhood and sisterhood of all. It includes an evaluation of the moral teachings of the present day Church. This evaluation shows that we have not repented nor been converted to the Gospel values even today. Epilogue follows to give my suggestions to liberate the victims and victimizers of this discriminatory system.

Throughout, my own personal search for meaning in the light of the Gospels, got mingled in this presentation. As my search was guided and answered by the struggling Dalit Christians in India, I call this, a Theology from a Dalit perspective. This book will move the hearts of all persons of good will and enable them to join in the on-going struggles of the oppressed for their liberation, it is hoped.

Many people of good will have abandoned religion as they rightly see in it a tool of oppression. Maybe, they too would be drawn to the true 'religion' of Jesus when they see how Jesus continues to inspire life into people in their struggle for a just human society.

It is also hoped that Jesus, rediscovered by the Dalits of India, would inspire confidence into the oppressed people everywhere in their struggle for liberation.

1. UNTOUCHABILITY IN THE BIBLE

We may touch a cat, we may touch a dog, we may touch any other animal, but the touch of these human beings is pollution.

G.K. Gokhale[1]

The practice of untouchability is not peculiar to India alone. Untouchability was practiced during the time of Jesus, too.

An instance: the Samaritan woman at Jacob's well ask Jesus:
Jn 4:9
... "How is it that you, a Jew, ask a drink of me, a woman of Samaria?" (Jews do not share things in common with Samaritans).

The Jews would not accept food or drink from the Samaritans. But Jesus surprises the Samaritan woman by asking her for water. The reporter, John, has added a comment confirming that the question posed by the woman was due to the practice of untouchability. Samaritans were segregated by the Jews.

The Samaritan woman was, in effect, asking Jesus: Where has your caste pride gone, now that you are thirsty?

Here, Jesus, the dominant caste man, is not harsh to her for the insult given to him. He seems to have taken it in his stride and

---

[1] As quoted by Albert M. Nevett, S.J., in article "Unchristian Things Done in the Name of Christianity", Vidyajoti, Vol XLV, No.6, June-July 1981, p.289 from "Six Great Missionaries", London 1930, p.161

continued a conversation with her, much to the scandal of his disciples. Some other passages that confirm this practice:

The words of Peter in his address to the people assembled in the house of Cornelius:
Act 10:28
. . . "You yourselves know that it is unlawful for a Jew to associate with or to visit a Gentile."

Question addressed to Peter:
Act 11:3
... "Why did you go to uncircumcised men and eat with them?"

A comment on Jesus for allowing a sinner 'to touch' him:
LK 7:39
. . . "If this man were a prophet, he would have known who and what kind of woman this is who is touching him - that she is a sinner."

All these are about practices of untouchability in the literal sense of the word.

The Jews appear to have practiced untouchability in all its various forms: No touching of persons considered impure, no entering of their houses, no acceptance of food or drink from their hands! What made the Jews practice untouchability among themselves, and between themselves and the rest of the world?

Biblical Factors Contributing to Untouchability

The practice of untouchability based on the division of humans as pure and impure is the fulcrum of the caste system. This evil system was a part of the world of the Jews at the time of Jesus. It is no surprise to learn that the law books that created this discriminatory distinction between people are nothing but the books of the Bible.

We have a law book in India, called the Manu Smriti, which had codified[2] the practice of untouchability. This Manu Smriti, sacred to the Hindus, was burnt by the great Dalit leader Dr. Ambedkar as an act of protest. What else should we do with law books that divide people? Books that make one race feel superior to another?

Does the Bible justify discrimination? Or, is there more to it than meets the eye? Let us follow the lead and see what was the basis for such a caste distinction in the Jewish world of Jesus.

Circumcision Factor

Circumcision not only cut the foreskin of a Jew, but it cut him off from the uncircumcised.

Genesis 17:10, 14

[10] This is my covenant, which you shall keep, between me and you and your offspring after you: Every male among you shall be circumcised.

[14] Any uncircumcised male who is not circumcised in the flesh of his foreskin **shall be cut off from his people**; he has broken my covenant. (*Emphasis added*)

It may be just a mark on his body. Yet, for a Jew, circumcision cuts him off from others with whom he might otherwise have related. It makes him conscious that he is superior to the uncircumcised as he has become related to God Himself through his circumcision. This law given by Moses forms the basis for this distinction between the Jews and other races.

That is why Peter could say to those gathered in the house of Cornelius that it was not **lawful** for him to enter the house of non-

---

[2] Frederick Herzog, Justice Church, Orbis Books, Second Print, 1981, p.31

Jews.

Pure and Impure Food

Let's examine the Bible to see if a purity-pollution division based on food habits has been used to differentiate between human beings. We do see many instructions in the Bible regarding what are pure and what are not in matters of food:

Lev 11: 10, 13, 24-26
[10] But anything in the seas or the streams that does not have fins and scales, of the swarming creatures in the waters and among all the other living creatures that are in the waters - they are detestable to you, and detestable they shall remain.
[13] These you shall regard as detestable among the birds. They shall not be eaten; they are an abomination: the eagle, the vulture, the osprey.
[24] By these you shall become unclean; whoever touches the carcass of any of them shall be unclean until the evening, [25] and whoever carries any part of the carcass of any of them shall wash his clothes and be unclean until the evening. [26] Every animal that has divided hoofs but is not cleft-footed or does not chew the cud is unclean for you; everyone who touches one of them shall be unclean.

The Bible does distinguish between clean and unclean food. It also divides people into the pure and the polluting by their food habits. Remember the words of Peter:

Acts 10:9-16
[9] About noon the next day, as they were on their journey and approaching the city, Peter went up on the roof to pray. [10] He became hungry and wanted something to eat; and while it was being prepared, he fell into a trance. [11] He saw the heaven opened and something like a large sheet coming down, being lowered to the ground by its four corners. [12] In it were all kinds of four-footed creatures and reptiles and birds of the air. [13] Then he heard a voice saying, "Get up,

Peter; kill and eat." [14] But Peter said, "By no means, Lord; for I have never eaten anything that is profane or unclean." [15] The voice said to him again, a second time, "What God has made clean, you must not call profane." [16] This happened three times, and the thing was suddenly taken up to heaven.

Peter had a trance before his first visit to the house of a non-Jew. He had never eaten anything unclean and the trance prepared him for his visit to the house of people he considered polluting. He had to face criticism from his fellow-Jewish Christians for his eating at Cornelius' house:

Acts 11:3
. . . "Why did you go to uncircumcised men and eat with them?"

In other words, how could the first Pope make himself impure by not practicing untouchability on non-Jews?

Is the Bible rational?

One might say that the Bible is not wholly unreasonable in dividing food into clean and unclean. It sounds reasonable to divide matter into eatable and not eatable based on the degree of its purity.

Let us consider for a moment the reasons given for considering certain animals unclean:

Lev 11:1-4, 7
The Lord spoke to Moses and Aaron, saying to them: [2] Speak to the people of Israel, saying: From among all the land animals, these are the creatures that you may eat. [3] Any animal that has divided hoofs and is cleft-footed and chews the cud - such you may eat. [4]. But among those that chew the cud or have divided hoofs, you shall not eat the following; the camel, for even though it chews the cud, it does not have divided hoofs; it is unclean to you.
[7] The pig, for even though it has divided hoofs and is cleft

footed, it does not chew the cud; it is unclean for you.

If the Bible says that the swine is unclean because it eats dirt, it would sound quite reasonable. But what if the swine is said to be unclean, because it does not chew the cud? In India, the swine does the job of scavenging in the open fields used as public toilets in the rural areas and, therefore, it is considered an unclean animal. That way, the swine should be doubly unclean if it chewed the cud! Such biblical distinctions of clean and unclean food do not seem to have any rational foundation. Perhaps, people who wanted the irrational distinctions between races have put them into the Bible to give a mystical and godly appearance to their mean desires?!

Pure and Impure Persons

The distinction between pure and impure does not stop with things eaten. It is extended to many other things and events that occur in the normal course of one's life:

Impure for reasons of nature:
Lev 15:19-24
[19] when a woman has a discharge of blood that is her regular discharge from her body, she shall be in her impurity for seven days, and whoever touches her shall be unclean until the evening. [20] Everything upon which she lies during her impurity shall be unclean; everything also upon which she sits shall be unclean. [21] Whoever touches her bed shall wash his clothes, and bathe in water, and be unclean until the evening. [22] Whoever touches anything upon which she sits shall wash his clothes, and bathe in water, and be unclean until the evening; [23] whether it is the bed or anything upon which she sits, when he touches it he shall be unclean until the evening. [24] If any man lies with her, and her impurity falls on him, he shall be unclean seven days; and every bed on which he lies shall be unclean.

Impure for reasons of sickness:
Lev 13:45-46

[45] The leper who has the leprous disease shall wear torn clothes and let the hair of his head be disheveled; and he shall cover his upper lip and cry, "Unclean, unclean." [46] He shall remain unclean as long as he has the disease; he is unclean. He shall live alone; his dwelling shall be outside the camp.

Impure for touching an impure thing/person:
Lev 5: 2-3

[2] Or when any of you touch any unclean thing - whether the carcass of an unclean beast or the carcass of unclean livestock or the carcass of an unclean swarming things - and are unaware of it, you have become unclean, and are guilty. [3] Or when you touch human uncleanness - any uncleanness by which one can become unclean - and are unaware of it, when you come to know it, you shall be guilty.

If the Jews could become unclean and guilty by touching the carcass of an animal, then they could never have removed dead animals from their midst. Either the Jews broke the commandments and removed dead animals away from their midst, or they had them removed by someone else, or they lived among dead animals.

In all probability, they had some people to do the 'dirty' job for them and they considered those who did the job low! Low, because they could clean up only after breaking the law thereby making themselves sinners. That comes very close to the Indian system of caste, where, often, the Dalits who do the scavenging works are made to feel inferior and polluting on account of the kind of jobs they are supposed to do. Let us examine what Jesus did with these laws. Did he accept or reject them?

2. JESUS AND UNTOUCHABILITY AMONG JEWS

Jews practiced untouchability among themselves. As if they belonged to a superior race, they practiced untouchability against all other races. In this chapter, what Jesus did with untouchability inside Jewish community is analyzed. What he did with this practice of Jews against the other races is to be taken up for an analysis in the next chapter.

Jesus and the Laws

Jewish consciousness of purity and pollution was rooted in the biblical laws. We begin our search with the question: What did Jesus do with the laws that divided people as pure and polluting?

Jesus' preaching about law:
Mt 5: 17-20
[17] "Do not think that I have come to abolish the law or the prophets; I have come not to abolish but to fulfil. [18] For truly I tell you, until heaven and earth pass away, not one letter, not one stroke of a letter, will pass from the law until all is accomplished. [19] Therefore, whoever breaks one of the least of these commandments, and teaches others to do the same, will be called least in the kingdom of heaven; but whoever does them and teaches them will be called great in the kingdom of heaven. [20] For I tell you, unless your righteousness exceeds that of the scribes and Pharisees, you will never enter the kingdom of heaven."

It looks as if Jesus accepted the Mosaic Law in all its totality. He claims to have come not to abolish but to fulfill them. But things are not clear when he says that one's righteousness should exceed that of the scribes and Pharisees...

Did Jesus mean that he wanted the law to be observed more rigorously than the scribes and Pharisees did? Or did he differ in his way of fulfilling the law? Did he believe in the biblical division of the pure and the polluting?

If the words of Jesus are not all that clear, let us hope we would find some clarity by looking at his actions:

Jesus' practice of law:

Mt 8: 1-4

[1]When Jesus had come down from the mountain, great crowds followed him; [2] and there was a leper who came to him and knelt before him, saying, "Lord, if you choose, you can make me clean." [3] He stretched out his hand and touched him, saying, "I do choose. Be made clean!" Immediately his leprosy was cleansed. [4] Then Jesus said to him, "See that you say nothing to anyone; but go, show yourself to the priest, and offer the gift that Moses commanded, as a testimony to them."

Jesus stretched out his hand and touched him. He did not consider the leper unclean, nor his touch polluting. He was not fulfilling Mosaic Law but breaking it when it teaches one to practice untouchability. That is definitely good news to the Dalits.

The leper broke the law on more than one count. He was not keeping himself away from others and he did not warn others by shouting "Unclean, unclean". Jesus did not find fault with him for not keeping this part of the law. That, too, is good news to the Dalits.

But Jesus' instructions to the leper make things a bit confusing. What did Jesus mean by bidding him not to tell anyone? After all, there was 'a great crowd following him' when he worked the miracle. He did not cure the leper in secret. After defying the

Mosaic law in public by his touching the leper, and after not condemning the leper for breaking the law, he is asking the cured person: to 'go to the priest, have yourself declared clean, and offer the gift that Moses ordered as a proof'. Did Jesus believe effecting a physical cure did not make a person sufficiently 'clean'? Why is he suddenly concerned with keeping the law that he just then broke?

This is what Moses commanded a person cured of leprosy to do:
Lev 14:2-5, 10
[2] This shall be the ritual for the leprous person at the time of his cleansing: He shall be brought to the priest; [3] the priest shall go out of the camp, and the priest shall make an examination. If the disease is healed in the leprous person, [4] the priest shall command that two living clean birds and cedar wood and crimson yam and hyssop be brought for the one who is to be cleansed. [5] The priest shall command that one of the birds be slaughtered over fresh water in an earthen vessel.
[10] On the eighth day he shall take two male lambs without blemish, and one ewe lamb in its first year without blemish, and a grain offering of three tenths of an ephah of choice flour mixed with oil, and one log of oil.

What did Jesus mean by asking the cured person to undertake this long route to purification? If Jesus believed a cured leper to be still unclean and polluting, he should not have touched him before curing him. Jesus is capable of curing the sick even from a distance. The instances of the cure often lepers, the centurion's servant, for instance, proves our point. If he would not consider a leper to be polluting then why should the man cured by leprosy get purified by observance of rituals dictated by the law?

Neither the teachings nor the practice of Jesus throw light on our search.

Frederick Herzog gives us some guidelines which might perhaps

help us in our search[3]:
1) Appreciate the fact of Jesus being a Jew.
2) Know the immediate pre-history of Church history.
3) The socio-cultural milieu of Jesus that he functioned in, and
4) The mainsprings of action provided to Jesus by his society.

Jesus: a Jew in his Socio-Cultural Milieu

Jesus was, first and foremost, a human being in flesh and blood. John says of Jesus: 'And the Word became flesh and lived among us ... '(Jn 1:14)

Jesus began his religious life the way every Jew of his time would begin, by being circumcised on the eighth day after birth, at the Jerusalem temple. The law of Moses influenced his life events and actions to a very great extent, especially during his infancy and childhood:

Lk 2: 21-24
[21] After eight days had passed, it was time to circumcise the child; and he was called Jesus, the name given by the angel before he was conceived in the womb. [22] When the time came for their purification according to the law of Moses, they brought him up to Jerusalem to present him to the Lord [23] (as it is written in the law of the Lord, "Every first-born male shall be designated as holy to the Lord"), [24] and they offered a sacrifice according to what is stated in the law of the Lord, "a pair of turtledoves or two young pigeons."

As an infant, Jesus was carried to the temple and was circumcised and redeemed with the offering of doves. At the age of twelve he was very much involved in listening to his religious teachers:

Lk 2: 46-48, 51-52
[46] After three days they found him in the temple, sitting

---

[3] Frederick Herzog, Justice Church, Orbis Books, Second Print, 1981, p.31

among the teachers, listening to them and asking them questions. [47] And all who heard him were amazed at his understanding and his answers. [48] When his parents saw him they were astonished; and his mother said to him, "Child, why have you treated us like this? Look, your father and I have been searching for you in great anxiety."
[51] Then he went down with them and came to Nazareth, and was obedient to them. His mother treasured all these things in her heart. [52] And Jesus increased in wisdom and in years, and in divine and human favor.

The above narration tells us that he went to the Jerusalem temple to celebrate the Passover as a matter of following the custom. There, at the age of twelve, he was sitting among teachers and listening to them and asking them questions. He was learning from the Jewish teachers. His learning process ended when his mother took him away. He was back home and was an obedient child to a devout Jewish mother.

That person, with such a devout childhood as his background, broke the law of untouchability by touching a leper implies quite a lot of change. His insistence on the leper to observe the purificatory obligations under the Mosaic Law is thus not surprising either. Perhaps he was changing gradually from the Jewish background.

As an adult, he would go to the extent of declaring that the temple had become a den of robbers and engage in driving them out. Hardly does anyone find Jesus listening to the teachers during his public life!

Mainsprings of Jesus' Action

As regards the age from twelve to thirty, we have a very insightful comment by Luke about Jesus:

> And Jesus increased in wisdom and in years, and in divine and human favor. (Lk 2:52)

If Jesus grew, then he changed. One cannot remain the same and still grow. Jesus' growth was not a matter related to his physical growth alone. He increased in wisdom, we are told. If one is born filled with wisdom, there would be no room for any growth in wisdom. Jesus, like all human beings, had to grow wiser.

Wisdom is born of experience of life and its struggles. On the life and struggles of Jesus before his public life, the Christian Community Bible makes an interesting comment:

> Being a son of an artisan, he grew up among simple, humble people. In addition, Jesus made an important decision when he was eighteen or twenty years old. He chose to remain a manual worker rather than enter a school for Teachers of the law. For these religious schools were open to all.

> Jesus could have begun his preaching as a qualified Teacher and he certainly would have found his helpers among the sincere teachers of the law, priests or Pharisees of good faith. But no, he preferred to educate himself through the worker's life with no other religious preparation than the teachings of the synagogue, with no other book than the book of life. Because of this, when the time came, he found his apostles among the common people, men who were simple but responsible people.[4]

The wisdom of Jesus was born out of his experience of life as a manual laborer. Of his early life as worker, we have practically nothing recorded in the Bible. We can only infer it from his teachings. The mainspring of action that provided Jesus his wisdom was that of his being a manual laborer. Therefore his wisdom could be expected to be colored by his experience as a worker in his society . . .

---

[4] Christian Community Bible, (hereafter referred to as CCB) Second Edition, Commentary on Mk 3: 13ff

Jesus' Awareness of the Agony of the Unemployed

Jesus, for instance, was aware of and, perhaps, experienced the problem of unemployment - of people waiting in the market places for someone to hire them for the day. He knew the importance, in the life of a daily wage-earner, of just getting hired for a job. It meant sustaining the life of his family.

Even today, it is not an uncommon experience for a Dalit to face starvation if he/she did not find someone to hire him/her for a job. On such a day, a starving Dalit usually seeks help from neighbors, to feed, if not oneself, one's children. When a whole village is left without any job for many days or weeks, then there is no possibility for Dalits to help one another. All of them starve along with their children.

A group of students of theology, wanted to ensure that their study should be meaningful to Dalit Christians. So, they first went to where the Dalits lived and collected theological questions as and when people aired them during their conversations.

In one village, the landless agricultural wage laborers, all Dalit Christians, were starving due to a drought that had brought all agricultural activity to a grinding halt. A question often found repeated by the Dalit Christians that time was: "Why did God create us at all? Did he create us only to starve and die? To see our children die of starvation before our very eyes?"

Such questions could not be answered with the wisdom of the traditional catechism that says: "God created us that we may know him, love him and serve him and thereby attain eternal life". These questions asked by starving Dalits were about God and **this** life . . .

Jesus the worker must have found the catechism he learnt in his temple and synagogue, not answering the questions raised by the life of workers. In Jesus' view, God's reign had to be different for a worker from the one taught by his religious teachers. He depicted his vision of the ideal world (Kingdom of God) through many parables that he composed and taught. His experience as worker had a mark on his parables.

An example:

Mt 20:1

For the kingdom of heaven is like a landowner who went out early in the morning to hire laborers for his vineyard …

Each time this landowner went out and saw some unemployed, he would ask them to go and join the workers he had hired. He did the same till evening. Naturally, when he paid full day's wages to those employed at late hours, those hired earlier expected something more.

Mt 20:11-15

[11] And when they received it, they grumbled against the landowner, [12] saying, 'these last worked only one hour, and you have made them equal to us who have borne the burden of the day and the scorching heat.' [13] But he replied to one of them, 'Friend, I am doing you no wrong; did you not agree with me for the usual daily wage? [14] Take what belongs to you and go; I choose to give to this last the same as I give to you. [15] Am I not allowed to do what I choose with what belongs to me? Or are you envious because I am generous?'

In speaking of the kingdom of God, the ideal world, Jesus places the daily wage laborers in a secure place of not being deprived of their daily food. The unemployed of the world need to be at least assured of their food particularly when they are unemployed for no fault of theirs. In God's kingdom, there shall be no hunger; all get full meal. This kind of thinking could come only to someone who has experienced the life of workers.

Looking at Religion and Bible from a Worker's Perspective

Jesus found that the religion of his time was blind to the problems of the workers, the jobless and the poor. The religious leaders did very little to remove the problem of unemployment. But they condemned those who got employed on a weekend saying that it was against law. Those who got employed on a weekend became 'sinners' - 'impure' and 'untouchable' - until they made purificatory offerings.

If one worked out of necessity on a week end, the reason is poverty. The poor worker became a poor sinner and, therefore, impure, for having worked on a week end. As a sinner, he/she had to spend on rituals to make himself/herself pure! Thus, the poor worker, because of the religious leaders' teaching became poorer. What a burden this religious teaching had become on the shoulders of the working class people! No wonder Jesus had so much to teach against the law of Sabbath.

He condemns his religious leaders for this:
> **Mt 23:4**
> "They tie up heavy burdens, hard to bear, and lay them on the shoulders of others; but they themselves are unwilling to lift a finger to move them."

Here, the very imagery Jesus picks out to depict the oppression is that of a manual laborer carrying a heavy burden.

Imagine the plight of one who is a shepherd by profession. He has to feed his sheep daily. Obviously, he cannot afford to let his flock starve because of his religious obligations. All shepherds necessarily worked on all Sabbath days, and became an untouchable class. They were lower in the social rank to those who could afford to rest on the Sabbath. Even for those who could afford to take rest on a Sabbath, the official interpretation given to the law made life impossible on a Sabbath day:

Jewish law prohibited all work on a Sabbath, because that was the day of the week consecrated by God. Yet the Jews reinforced and added to the prohibitions of past generations, to the extent of not even allowing people to light a fire, or walk more than 1,000 paces or pick wheat, or heal the sick on the Sabbath.[5]

The worker, on a rest day, cannot afford to take care of his medical or any personal needs. For that he/she should take another day off! Thus the Sabbath law created out of poor workers and the shepherds a whole set of impure castes. The Sabbath became yet another foundation for the hierarchical division of Jewish society.

Cost Involved in Keeping/Making Oneself Clean

The law required of a Jew to make costly offerings in the temple for making one pure. It prescribed practices like ritual bathing in water when one came in touch with what the law defined as defiling.

The Christian Community Bible, in its commentary on Mark 7:14ff, says:
> If contaminated even by no fault of his own, the person had to purify himself, usually with water, sometimes paying for sacrifices.[6]

In the book of Leviticus, we find Yahweh telling Moses and Aaron to instruct the Israelites regarding women who have delivered babies:
Lev 12:6-8
[6] And when the days of her purification are completed, whether for a son or for a daughter, she shall bring to the

---

[5] Ibid on: Mk3

[6] Ibid on Mk 7: 14 ff

priest at the entrance of the tent of meeting a lamb in its first year for a burnt offering, and a pigeon or a turtledove for a sin offering. [7] He shall offer it before the Lord, and make atonement on her behalf; then she shall be clean from the flow of her blood. This is the law for her who bears a child, male or female. [8] If she cannot afford a sheep, she shall take two turtledoves or two pigeons, one for a burnt offering and the other for a sin offering; and the priest shall make atonement on her behalf, and she shall be clean.

Every birth of a child involved, for the whole family, a journey to Jerusalem and making offerings just to make themselves clean. We can imagine what a burden it would have become on the people, particularly the daily wage laborers.

Had not Joseph and Mary been to Jerusalem, to purify Mary and circumcise Jesus? All these were done in obedience to the commandment given by the Lord to the people of Israel through Moses and Aaron. What of those people who could not afford to make the journey and bring offerings prescribed by law? Are they to remain untouchable sinners to the end?

Jesus the Thinker

Jesus must have wondered at the burden placed on workers by the Bible. Is not the God who gave such instructions the Father of all these people? Does he not love them? Then, why in God's name is the burden imposed on the poor?

His reflections on the plight of the poor workers should have taken him through a rereading of the Bible to verify the veracity of the teachings of his priests. He must have read passages dealing with the commandments of Yahweh. He must have come across passages in the Bible that condemn such ritualistic practices.

The Bible that gives instructions about offerings in the book of

Leviticus is also saying, for instance, in the seventh chapter of the book of Jeremiah, that those passages dealing with sacrifices are not from God! Some clever people have interpolated the Bible itself for their own benefit. The Bible itself says that Jesus has definitely read this passage since he quotes a verse from the same seventh chapter of Jeremiah. That, when he drives out the merchants from the Temple.

Jer 7:21-23
> [21] Thus says the Lord of hosts, the God of Israel: Add your burnt offerings to your sacrifices, and eat the flesh. [22] For in the day that I brought your ancestors out of the land of Egypt, I did not speak to them or command them concerning burnt offerings and sacrifices. [23] But this command I gave them, "Obey my voice, and I will be your God, and you shall be my people; and walk only in the way that I command you, so that it may be well with you."

Apparently, Jesus must have found himself confronted by two different images of Yahweh: One hungering for animal sacrifices, and the other, a loving and caring father.

Jesus must have deeply reflected and gone through a period of confusion. (Maybe, this confusion is what is reflected in the episode of his curing the leper). Eventually, as we will see shortly, he opts to take prophet Jeremiah's rendering of Yahweh to be authentic and that of Leviticus as bogus.

In Jesus' opinion, Yahweh could not have commanded these burnt offerings and sacrifices. He is a loving father. He would not place such a heavy burden on His children. Besides, He does not eat the offerings. It is the priests who eat the goats offered.

God gave the Ten Commandments, according to Jeremiah, not for any pleasure He derived in prohibiting His children any pleasures. It was not the forbidden acts but what the acts did to His children that made Him give the commandments. Nor were the commandments any expression of God's personal desire to play a dictator to His people. He gave them because He wanted to ensure the wellbeing of all His children, as becoming of a loving father. Murder, bearing false witness, adultery and such other acts affect Yahweh just because it affects the well-being of His children.

Jr 7:23
Walk only in the way that I command you, so that it may be well with you.

Jesus opts for the prophetic version of Yahweh and condemns the sacrifices and other purificatory rituals. If the sacrifices and rituals found a place in the Bible, they originated from vested interests, and not from God. Jesus would quote the authority of Isaiah to prove his point:

Mark 7:5-8
[5] So the Pharisees and the scribes asked him, "Why do your disciples not live according to the tradition of the elders, but eat with defiled hands?" [6] He said to them, "Isaiah prophesied rightly about you hypocrites, as it is written, 'This people honors me with their lips, But their hearts are far from me; [7] **in vain do they worship me, teaching human precepts as doctrines.'** [8] You abandon the commandment of God and hold to human tradition."

This quotation from Isaiah, chapter twenty nine, talks of replacing the wisdom of Jewish wise men!

Isaiah 29: 13-14
[13] The Lord said:
Because this people draw near with their mouths
and honor me with their lips,
while their hearts are far from me, and their worship of
me is a human commandment learned by rote;
[14] so I will again do amazing things with this people, shocking and amazing.
The wisdom of their wise shall perish,
and the discernment of the discerning shall be hidden.

Here, the Lord of Isaiah is condemning the wisdom of the wise. It is not only because it's human origin but also because it has been learnt by rote. Wisdom should come from life experience of people. Therefore, the other kind of wisdom shall perish! No wonder, this wisdom of rote went against the wisdom born of the praxis of Jesus.

If the well-being of his children was the reason for giving the commandments, then God could not have demanded costly sacrifices. They were not helping the well-being of the poor workers.

Rationalist God

Jesus must have found his reading of the first chapter of Isaiah confirming his search for the meaning of the sacrifices and ceremonial customs going on endlessly in the temple - endlessly burdening the worker:
Isaiah 1: 11 - 18
[11] What to me is the multitude of your sacrifices? Says the Lord;
I have had enough of burnt offerings of rams and the fat of fed beasts;
I do not delight in the blood of bulls, or of lambs, or of goats.
[12] When you come to appear before me who asked this from your hand?
Trample my courts no more;
[13] bringing offerings is futile;
incense is an abomination to me.
New moon and Sabbath and calling of convocation –
I cannot endure solemn assemblies with iniquity.
[14] Your new moons and your appointed festivals
my soul hates; they have become a burden to me,
I am weary of bearing them.
[15] When you stretch out your hands,
I will hide my eyes from you;
even though you make many prayers,

I will not listen; your hands are full of blood.
¹⁶ Wash yourselves; make yourselves clean;
remove the evil of your doings from before my eyes;
cease to do evil,
¹⁷ learn to do good; seek justice, rescue the oppressed, defend the orphan, plead for the widow.
¹⁸ Come now, let us argue it out, says the Lord:
though your sins are like scarlet, they shall be like snow; though they are red like crimson, they shall become like wool.

Such passages as these could have clarified; for Jesus, Yahweh's stand regarding what he really wants of his people. Verse 17 above explains verse 16: Doing good and seeking justice clean people. The God of Isaiah is a rationalist! He invites people to reason out things with him!

Jesus holds on to this rational Yahweh as his God. Not the Yahweh who demands offerings and sacrifices through the law books of the Bible but the Yahweh who condemns them through the books of the prophets. Only this Yahweh can be the hope of the poor. The other is the oppressor of the poor. God is not happy with the sacrifices. God does not believe that one could make oneself pure by observing rituals in His temple! He would rather have His people seek justice, do good, correct oppression, defend the fatherless and the widow, if they want to be clean. That is the essence of His commandments which He wants His children to obey. And obedience would make them shine as snow, as wool!

Jesus accepts this rationalist Yahweh when he says of his teachers:

Mt 23:23-24
²³ Woe to you, scribes and Pharisees, hypocrites! For you tithe mint, dill and cumin, and have neglected the weightier matters of the law: justice and mercy and faith. It is these you ought to have practiced, without neglecting the others.
²⁴ You blind guides! You strain out a gnat but swallow a

camel!

The laws on purity, rituals and sacrifices would, all put together, weigh a gnat compared to justice and mercy and faith which would weigh a camel. Jesus was more worried about the lack of mercy, faith and justice, which is in the prophetic tradition of thinking.

In the same spirit of his Yahweh of the prophets, Jesus would take the whip and drive out the vendors from the Temple.

Jn 2:13-16
[13] The Passover of the Jews was near, and Jesus went up to Jerusalem. [14] In the temple he found people selling cattle, sheep, and doves, and the money changers seated at their tables. [15] Making a whip of cords, he drove all of them out of the temple, both the sheep and the cattle. He also poured out the coins of the money changers and overturned their tables. [16] He told those who were selling the doves, "Take these things out of here! Stop making my Father's house a market-place!"

Luke gives us the words used by Jesus on this occasion:

Lk 19:45-46
[45] Then he entered the temple and began to drive out those who were selling things there; [46] and he said, "It is written, 'My house shall be a house of prayer'; but you have made it a den of robbers."

How much Jesus was influenced by the prophet Jeremiah could be seen from the following:

Jer.7:11
Has this house, which is called by my name, become a den of robbers in your sight?

The vendors were selling goods to help people obey the commandment of God regarding the temple offerings. By driving them away, Jesus is preaching the Yahweh of the prophets who does not need the sacrifices.

One wonders what Joseph would have done when he arrived after a long journey with Mary and baby Jesus if there were no one selling pigeons in the temple. He would have had to go and fetch two young pigeons from the wilderness leaving Mary and baby Jesus at the doorsteps of the temple, or take lessons first on how to catch pigeons without harming them!

By attempting to stop the ritualistic form of worship in the temple, Jesus is telling us:
1) That one should disobey the Bible when one finds any commandment contained in it going against the spirit of Yahweh of the prophets.
2) That we should be concerned more with justice, mercy and faith than anything else to keep ourselves pure.
3) That there is no legitimacy in dividing people as pure and impure based on the scriptural injunctions regarding the rituals one should practice.
4) Sacrifices cannot obtain God's forgiveness. The love of the Father forgives sins.
5) What is needed is to go back to Him with confidence in His love.

Law Redefined

Jesus would go to the length of redefining the law itself. For instance, about the Sabbath, he would say:
> **Mk 2:27**
> 'The Sabbath was made for humankind, not humankind for the Sabbath.'

Sabbath is first a holiday. Its holiness is in its being a holiday for the worker. That is the theology from the perspective of Jesus the worker.

The Clean and the Unclean Redefined

Going far beyond, and contrary to, the definitions given in the book of law, Jesus ventures to give an alternative very much in style with the Yahweh of the poor who constantly invites people to be reasonable:

> **Mark 7:14-23**
> [14] Then he called the crowd again and said to them, "Listen to me, all of you, and understand: [15] there is nothing outside a person that by going in can defile, but the things that come out are what defile.[16] [17] When he had left the crowd and entered the house, his disciples asked him about the parable. [18] He said to them, "Then do you also fail to understand? Do you not see that whatever goes into a person from outside cannot defile, [19] since it enters, not the heart but the stomach, and goes out into the sewer?" (Thus he declared all foods clean.) [20] And he said, "It is what comes out of a person that defiles. [21] For it is from within, from the human heart, that evil intentions come: fornication, theft, murder, [22] adultery, avarice, wickedness, deceit, licentiousness, envy, slander, pride, folly. [23] All these evil things come from within, and they defile a person."

This teaching of Jesus on matters regarding eating habits goes very much against the commandments contained in the book of Leviticus; that is, against the biblical teachings regarding clean and unclean foods.

Mark, in verse 19 above, makes the purpose of Jesus' teaching here explicit by his comment: "Thus he declared all foods clean." It is the question of division of food into clean/unclean that is discussed here and Jesus has declared everything eatable clean. By that, he has ended also the division of people as clean and unclean based on food habits, a division that leads to the practice of untouchability.

Jesus' Way of Fulfilling the Law and the Prophets

Is there not an apparent or obvious contradiction between the laws and the prophets? Can we simply say that we will keep the prophets and drop the law books? How does Jesus respond?

The Sermon on the Mount:
> **Mt 7:12**
> "In everything do to others as you would have them do to you; for this is the law and the prophets."

Does not Jesus see any contradiction between the law and the prophets?

Jesus does not say there is no contradiction. From the angle of loving one's neighbor as oneself, there should not be any contradiction. For him, if one has done to his/her neighbor what one would have wished others do to him/her, then necessarily the law and the prophets are fulfilled. It may not be true of every passage of the law and the prophets. What is important is doing to others what one would love others to do for oneself.

This very golden rule taught by Jesus is taken almost literally from the book of law, much of which he had condemned as creation of vested interests. He has located a simple key from the same book, a key with which one should judge the law and the prophets.
> **Lev 19:17-18**
> [17] "You shall not hate in your heart anyone of your kin; you shall reprove your neighbor, or you will incur guilt yourself. [18] You shall not take vengeance or bear a grudge against any of your people, but you shall love your neighbor as yourself: I am the Lord."

Can there be any practice of untouchability among human beings, if all were to abide by this law? Would anyone wish others to treat him/her as an untouchable?

Believers think that Jesus being 'the Son of God' could redefine things told in the Bible itself, and that, however, they themselves do not have that freedom. On the contrary Jesus invites his followers to use their brains and be bold enough to make decisions. It was not for any heavenly privilege enjoyed by Jesus that he took the liberty to make changes in the law and its interpretations.

People at the time of Jesus thought that it did need an authorization from above to teach the way Jesus taught defying the dictates of biblical laws. How could a laborer, that Jesus was, preach against practices coming straight out of the Bible?

Mt 13:54-56

[54] He came to his hometown and began to teach the people in their synagogue, so that they were astounded and said, "Where did this man get this wisdom and these deeds of power? [55] Is not this the carpenter's son? Is not his mother called Mary? And are not his brothers James and Joseph and Simon and Judas? [56] And are not all his sisters with us? Where then did this man get all this?"

They would have believed Jesus if he had proved his authority. Jesus refuses to give them any sign of authority. He appealed instead, to their reasoning capabilities which he thought people had in abundance.

Asked for a sign from heaven to prove his authority, Jesus replied:

Lk 12:54-57

[54] He also said to the crowds, "When you see a cloud rising in the west, you immediately say, 'It is going to rain'; and so it happens. [55] And when you see the south wind blowing, you say, 'There will be scorching heat'; and it happens. [56] You hypocrites! You know how to interpret the appearance of earth and sky, but why do you not know how to interpret the present time? [57] "And why do you not judge for yourselves what is right?"

Jesus invites one to use one's brains: Judge for oneself what is right. Doing to others what one would like to do to oneself - that is the principle and foundation on which all the laws and prophets stand. And no practice of untouchability, no practice of segregation can stand on this foundation.

Jesus had time and again changed the interpretation of biblical laws precisely on the score of the laws having become anachronistic. They were not in step with the times. They were perhaps alright for olden days when people were less civilized, less reasonable, and hence hard-hearted.

He claimed that he had not come to abolish the laws but to fulfil them. His way of fulfilling the law was by refusing to be bound blindly to them, but interpreting them according to the signs of the times. Interpreting laws this way is a freedom and responsibility given to all by Jesus. This is how he does the interpretation:

Mt 5:17, 21,22,27,28

[17] "Do not think that I have come to abolish the law or the prophets; I have come not to abolish but to fulfill ...

[21] "You have heard that it was said to those of ancient times, 'You shall not murder'; and 'whoever murders shall be liable to judgement.' [22] But I say to you that if you are angry with a brother or sister, you will be liable to judgement; and if you insult a brother or sister, you will be liable to the council; and if you say, 'You fool,' you will be liable to the hell of fire. [27] "You have heard that it was said, 'You shall not commit adultery.' [28] But I say to you that everyone who looks at a woman with lust has already committed adultery with her in his heart."

Changing times have to keep challenging us to a deeper understanding of the commandment of love. How anachronistic it is for the Church to have a caste system today when the secular world accepts the principle of equality of all! To have a male dominated Church when the whole world has accepted gender equality in every sphere of life! To have a monarchical Church when the world has developed democratic forms of governance!

Jesus the Revolutionary

Giving newer definitions of laws, Jesus not only preached them, he also put them into practice. Which means that he rejected or broke laws and their interpretations when they contradicted his newer definition.

Jesus, wanting to establish justice, mercy and faith, rejected the practice of untouchability and worked towards establishing equality among the Jews.

Contrary to the demands of the law, he 'polluted' himself in public and scandalized the guardians of the law. He touched the untouchables of Israel.

Mt 8:2-3
2 and there was a leper who came to him and knelt before him, saying, "Lord, if you choose, you can make me clean." 3 He stretched out his hand and touched him, saying, "I do choose. Be made clean!" Immediately his leprosy was cleansed.

When touched by the women suffering hemorrhage, Jesus did not at all go in for purification rituals like washing himself and his clothes in water and so on, as per the dictates of the law:

Mt 9:22
Jesus turned, and seeing her he said, "Take heart, daughter; your faith has made you well."

What a scandal he should have caused by those words and action to the law-abiding citizens of Israel!

He associated with 'untouchable sinners' by eating with them to the scandal of the 'pure':

Mt 9:10-11
10 And as he sat at dinner in the house, many tax collectors and sinners came and were sitting with him and his disciples.

[11] When the Pharisees saw this, they said to his disciples, "Why does your teacher eat with tax collectors and sinners?"

And again when he chose to go to the house of Zacchaeus:

Lk 19:7

All who saw it began to grumble and said, "He has gone to be the guest of one who is a sinner."

He touches the polluting dead body of a girl:

Mt 9:24-25

[24] He said, "Go away; for the girl is not dead but sleeping." And they laughed at him. [25] But when the crowd had been put outside, he went in and took her by the hand, and the girl got up.

He could be comfortable when touched by a sinner:

Lk 7:39

Now when the Pharisee who had invited him saw it he said to himself, 'If this man were a prophet, he would have known who and what kind of woman this is who is touching him - which she is a sinner. '

Jesus not only allows her to touch him but even argues that the show of affection for him expressed by her touch, kisses etc., is the reason for her many sins being forgiven:

Lk 7:44-47

[44] Then turning toward the woman, he said to Simon, "Do you see this woman? I entered your house, you gave me no water for my feet, but she has bathed my feet with her tears and dried them with her hair. [45] You gave me no kiss, but from the time I came in she has not stopped kissing my feet. [46] You did not anoint my head with oil, but she has anointed my feet with ointment. [47] Therefore, I tell you, her sins, which were many, have been forgiven; hence she has shown great love. But the one to whom little is forgiven, loves little."

Contrary to what the Pharisees felt, Jesus claimed to have been purified by the touch of the woman! By her washing and anointing him.

The urgent mission of Jesus is to touch the untouchables and to be touched by them. He would break the law of Sabbath and cure a person on a Sabbath rather than protecting the law by postponing the cure by a day.

> **Mark 3:4**
> Then he said to them, "Is it lawful to do good or to do harm on the Sabbath, to save life or to kill?"

The Sabbath was killing people! It was doing them harm. It was helping some to feel superior to the others and it was promoting the practice of segregation. Therefore the law of Sabbath could be disobeyed.

Jesus would quote from the Bible itself the justification for such disobedience to the biblical law!

> **Mark 2:23-27**
> [23] One Sabbath he was going through the grain fields; and as they made their way his disciples began to pluck heads of grain. [24] The Pharisees said to him, "Look, why are they doing what is not lawful on the Sabbath?" [25] And he said to them, "Have you never read what David did when he and his companions were hungry and in need of food? [26] He entered the house of God, when Abiatha was high priest, and ate the bread of the Presence, which it is not lawful for any but the priests to eat, and he gave some to his companions."
> [27] Then he said to them, "The Sabbath was made for humankind, and not humankind for the Sabbath;"

The argument of Jesus here, is that David and his men being in need was reason enough to justify breaking a biblical law. If a king's hunger proved to be a sufficient reason to break Mosaic Law, the same could very well be broken to appease the hunger of a poor man/woman.

It is worthwhile to note here that Jesus remembered an apparently uneventful passage in the Bible and uses it so well against his enemies. Unless one reads the Bible with a view to find an answer to the question 'What does Bible say to the hungry people?' one would miss the passage Jesus quoted here in his defense. Definitely, Jesus had read his Bible with the eyes of people who know hunger from experience.

Law and Ethics

It looks a bit scandalous that Jesus interpreted laws from the situation of the poor. We can appreciate Jesus better when we consider the following observation of the author of the Indian Penal Code on the relation between law and ethics.

The Indian Penal Code is a set of laws that defines acts that are not lawful and the punishment for one who breaks the laws. After drafting the Indian Penal Code, Lord McCauley, introduces the Code thus:

" ... We cannot admit that a Penal Code is by any means to be considered a body of ethics, that the legislature ought to punish acts merely because those acts are immoral, or that, because an act is not punished at all, it follows that the legislature considers that act as innocent. Many things which are not punishable are morally worse than many things which are punishable. The man who treats a generous benefactor with gross ingratitude and insolence deserves more severe reprehension than the man who aims a blow in a passion, or breaks a window in a frolic; yet we have punishment for assault and mischief, and none for ingratitude. The rich man who refuses a mouthful of rice to save a fellow-creature from death may be a far worse man than the starving wretch who snatches and devours the rice; yet we punish the latter for theft, and we do not punish the former for hardheartedness . . ."[7]

Jesus Risking Life for Breaking Laws

Jesus approaches the issue with the very principle he was teaching all to follow: whatever you wish that men would do to you, do so to them. The corollary of this teaching is that whatever good you believe you can do to your fallen sheep on a Sabbath, you should all the more do for human beings in need:

Mt 12:11-14

[11] He said to them, "Suppose one of you has only one sheep and it falls into a pit on the Sabbath; will you not lay hold of it and lift it out? [12] How much more valuable is a human being than a sheep! So it is lawful to do good on the Sabbath." [13] Then he said to the man, "Stretch out your hand." He stretched it out, and it was restored, as sound as the other. [14] But the Pharisees went out and conspired against him, how to destroy him.

Risking his Reputation

Talking of the treatment given him by his compatriots, Jesus says:

Mt 11:19

The Son of Man came, eating and drinking, and they say, 'Look, a glutton and a drunkard, a friend of tax collectors and sinners!'

A man who could not control his appetite and avoid dinners with polluting sinners, could very well have appeared to be a glutton and a drunkard. Jesus enjoyed good food and the company of sinful and dirty people as well.

---

[7] From "Draft Penal Code Note Q.", p.174, as quoted in "Criminal Law Cases and Materials", by K. D. Gaur, Bombay, 1975, N. M. Tripathi P. Ltd., p.4

Subverting the Hierarchy of Values

Jesus shook the foundations of the division of human beings into the pure and the impure.

He would allow and use a pure-impure division among human beings on one count alone. That is, against those very people who divided people into the pure and the polluting. Such persons should be avoided to protect oneself from the poison of their dirty morality.

Thus, talking of the Pharisees, Jesus could say that they were a polluting lot.

Lk 11:44
Woe to you! For you are like unmarked graves, and people walk over them without realizing it.

The Christian Community Bible is more explicit in its rendering of the same verse:
"A curse on you for you are like tombstones of the dead which can hardly be seen; people don't notice them and make themselves unclean by stepping on them."

That Jesus was uttering these words while at table in the house of a Pharisee who was playing host to him shows us how deeply involved Jesus was in his commitment to the abolition of untouchability.

Lk 11:37-40
[37] While he was speaking, a Pharisee invited him to dine with him; so he went in and took his place at the table. [38] The Pharisee was amazed to see that he did not first wash before dinner. [39] Then the Lord said to him, 'Now you Pharisees clean the outside of the cup and of the dish, but inside you are full of greed and wickedness. [40] You fools! Did not the one who made the outside make the inside also?'

This is the same Jesus who also said elsewhere:

Mt 5:22

But I say to you that if you are angry with a brother or sister, you will be liable to judgement; and if you insult a brother or sister, you will be liable to the council; and if you say, 'You fool,' you will be liable to the hell of fire.

Obviously, the Pharisees who practiced purity-pollution ideas on people were not considered by Jesus as his brothers! Is that the reason why Jesus called them "fools" after preaching against calling one's brother a fool?

Thus, to destroy the practice of untouchability, Jesus would go to any length: even allow himself to be counted a dishonest preacher who did not practice what he preached. He would rather choose hell (which he himself said is reserved for those who call their brothers 'fools') than avoid calling Pharisees 'fools' for practicing ritual purity.

Jesus completes the process of subversion of purity-pollution division, by putting the so-called impure sinners above the pure Pharisees:

Mt 21:31

"Which of the two did the will of his father?" They said, "The first." Jesus said to them, "Truly I tell you, the tax collectors and the prostitutes are going into the kingdom of God ahead of you."

And who are the tax collectors and sinners? Socially, they are the people ranked lowest among the Jews: the out-castes within the Jewish society:

The Gospel speaks about the publicans or the tax collectors, who served the foreign powers. For, Jesus' nation was under the domination of the Roman Empire and the tax collectors were Jews who worked for foreigners. Patriots considered them traitors. The people knew they filled their pockets; even the beggars refused to receive from the publicans. Yet Jesus did not condemn them but chose one of them, Levi, as one of his apostles of whom the majority were committed patriots.

Jesus not only preached revolutionary ideas going contrary to the dictates and interpretation of the Bible, but he practiced a counter-culture of treating everyone equally. He would choose a man, from whom even beggars would refuse to accept alms, to be his apostle...

Jesus And Untouchability

3. JESUS AND UNTOUCHABILITY AGAINST OTHER RACES

We saw that Jesus grew up in the Jewish world. It is normal to expect a growing child to be affected by the world-view of the culture in which it is brought up.

As the Jewish world-view was one polarized between the circumcised and the uncircumcised, we could expect Jesus to have acquired a vision of a world characterized by the same polarities. We shall see shortly that his experience and wisdom gained by his life as a laborer was not sufficient to help him get out of the prejudices Jews nurtured against other races.

Jesus' Racial Prejudice Shows

Time and again we could see his prejudice regarding non-Jews showing itself:

Mt 6:7-8

[7] "When you are praying, do not heap up empty phrases as the Gentiles do; for they think that they will be heard because of their many words. [8] Do not be like them, for your Father knows what you need before you ask him."

This clearly indicates the prejudice Jesus had against non-Jews. There is no need for him to have included the phrase "as the Gentiles do". The statement would have made sense all the same. But the words "Do not be like them!" makes his prejudice even more explicit. Isolating the Jews from the non-Jews by a command 'do not be like them' does not speak well of a founder of a new world religion. Jesus is yet to get out of his racial prejudice?

Jesus lets his prejudice show again when he says:

Mt 6:31-33

[31] "Therefore do not worry, saying, 'What will we eat?' or 'What will we drink?' or 'What will we wear?' [32] For it is the Gentiles who strive for all these things; and indeed your heavenly Father knows that you need all these things. [33] But strive first for the kingdom of God and his righteousness, and all these things will be given to you as well."

Here too, his teaching without the verse 32 would have made perfect sense. If Jesus added it for emphasizing his point, he did it by revealing his racial prejudice! It is definitely not the Gentiles alone who strive for all these things: food, drink and clothing. They are the basic needs of all human beings, including the Jews. If the heavenly Father will take care of these needs for Jews only, how could he be the Father of all?

One who taught the world the prayer 'Our Father' is seen here using the word 'Your Father' in an exclusively Jewish sense.

To the Lost Sheep of Israel Only

Jesus initially understood his mission and the mission of his chosen apostles as that directed exclusively to the Jews.

Mt 10:5-8

[5] These twelve Jesus sent out with the following instructions: "Go nowhere among the Gentiles, and enter no town of the Samaritans [6] but go rather to the lost sheep of the house of Israel. [7] As you go, proclaim the good news, 'The kingdom of heaven has come near.' [8] Cure the sick, raise the dead, cleanse the lepers, cast out demons. You received without payment; give without payment ..."

Jesus wanted the preaching of the Good News of the Kingdom limited to the land of Israel. The ministries of healing, driving out devils etc., were not to reach the non-Jews. His world was restricted to Israel.

If his disciples continued to take this command of the Lord seriously and kept away from the non-Jews, we would not surely have the Church we have today. Either Jesus changed his mind at some point of time, or the disciples forgot this command of Jesus not to have dealings with the non-Jews. And non-Jews, let us keep in mind, were all considered untouchables.

Some Church leaders claim that the Father of Jesus had a plan of history to work through Jews first. That would mean that the Father was either racially prejudiced or that he was not aware at an earlier phase, that he was the Father of all people.

It is more probable that, as a devout Jew, Jesus shared the prejudice of his fellow-men.

Later, after his murder and resurrection, Jesus, in fact, gave a very different command to his disciples:

Mt 28:19
"Go therefore and make disciples of all nations, baptizing them ..."

This implies that somewhere during his ministry, Jesus had changed his world-view. So much so, what he had once explicitly forbidden his disciples to do, he would now command them to do.

One of the occasions that changed his outlook could be the encounter with the centurion.

Encounter with the Centurion

Jesus was on his way to the house of the centurion when he was intervened by a message from the centurion which surprised him:

Lk 7:6-9
[6] " . . . Lord, do not trouble yourself, for I am not worthy to

have you come under my roof; [7] therefore I did not presume to come to you. But only speak the word, and let my servant be healed. [8] For I also am a man set under authority, with soldiers under me; and I say to one, 'Go,' and he goes, and to another, 'Come,' and he comes, and to my slave, 'Do this,' and the slave does it." [9] When Jesus heard this he was amazed at him, and turning to the crowd that followed him, he said, **"I tell you, not even in Israel have I found such faith."**

Jesus was, indeed, surprised that a non-Jew exhibited more faith than a Jew. Did Jesus believe faith to be a monopoly of the Jews? His words of exclamation come as a pointer to the collapse of his world-view, of the neat distinction of the world into the believing Israel and the non-believing non-Jews.

The decision of Jesus to go to the house of a non-Jewish centurion came as a response to the recommendation of his Jewish elders. The centurion, an untouchable foreigner by Jewish standards, had not dared to invite him, in the first place.

He had sent Jewish elders to go to Jesus and plead his case. Maybe, he suspected Jesus might not help non-Jews that easily. The words of recommendation by the Jewish elders confirm that suspicion:

Lk 7:4-5
[4] ... "He is worthy of having you do this for him, [5] for he loves our people, and it is he who built our synagogue for us."

This recommendation in blunt terms would read: 'Though he is not a Jew, he is our well-wisher and benefactor and therefore you could treat him favorably with your Jewish hands!'

The centurion was not exhibiting any deep sense of spiritual humility when he said he was not worthy to have Jesus under his roof. His was an expression of his low social status given him in Israel. He was concerned to protect Jesus from the pollution he would cause himself were he to enter his house.

That is why, when the centurion heard that Jesus was coming to his house, he rushed his friends to Jesus with the words: "Lord do not trouble yourself, for I am not worthy to have you come under my roof; therefore, I did not presume to come to you."

The Christian Community Bible has the following commentary regarding Jesus' encounter with the centurion, under Lk 7, 1ff:

> The captain of a foreign army had earned the esteem of the Jews. The amazing thing was not that he should have contributed to the building of the synagogue, but rather that the Jews should have accepted it from him. He must have been a good man. But he knew the Jew's prejudices too well to have dared to personally approach this Jesus of whom they spoke. Indeed, up to what point did Jesus share his compatriots' pride? Would he respond to the petition of a Roman official?
>
> The centurion was really troubled: would Jesus consent to go to a pagan's house and 'become impure?' And the captain goes one step further: Jesus does not have to come to his house . . .

That was why he was sending his Jewish friends to Jesus.

Prejudice Overcome by Experience-Based Insights

The exclamation of Jesus 'Not even in Israel' is an expression of the shock he received in the wake of his encounter with the faith of a non-Jew. An untouchable non-Jew had effectively challenged the world-view of Jesus. Such an encounter could shatter a person to pieces and turn his world upside down.

Was not Jesus too shaken out of his narrow world-view by his experience in his ministry?

There could have been many such events in the life of Jesus that broadened his narrow Jewish world-view. The manifestation of the faith of the non-Jewish centurion is one such.

Besides expressing his surprise, Jesus comes out with a statement of his own conversion:

Mt 8:11-12

[11] "I tell you, many will come from east and west and will eat with Abraham and Isaac and Jacob in the kingdom of heaven, [12] while the heirs of the kingdom will be thrown into the outer darkness, where there will be weeping and gnashing of teeth."

More than the kingdom getting opened for many from east and west, it was Jesus' world-view that got widened that day. More than being an acknowledgement of the centurion's faith, this passage proclaims a faith experience of Jesus. It is no more that only the lost sheep of Israel are to be cared for, but all the children of the world; all are invited and eligible to take their seats at the dining table of God.

Another incident that shook Jesus was the case of the Canaanite woman.

Encounter with the Canaanite Woman

Mt 15:22-28

[22] Just then a Canaanite woman from that region came out and started shouting, "Have mercy on me, Lord, Son of David; my daughter is tormented by a demon." [23] But he did not answer her at all. And his disciples came and urged him, saying, "Send her away, for she keeps shouting after us." [24] He answered, "I was sent only to the lost sheep of the house of Israel." [25] But she came and knelt before him, saying, "Lord, help me." [26] He answered, "It is not fair to take the children's food and throw it to the dogs." [27] She said, "Yes, Lord, yet even dogs eat the crumbs that fall from their

masters' table." [28] Then Jesus answered her, "Woman, great is your faith! Let it be done for you as you wish." And her daughter was healed instantly.

Christian Community Bible comments:
> During the centuries before Christ, God communicated only with the Jews and he let other nations grope for him. This was part of God's wise and merciful plan, but because of the special treatment, the Jews began to think that the pagans were unworthy in the eyes of God; the Jews were the sons or children and the pagans were to be looked down upon as no more than dogs.
>
> Jesus answers the afflicted woman repeating this well-known scornful saying of the Jews. He said this to test this woman's faith: in effect, would she insist when it appeared that even God would reject her?

We learn from the commentary quoted here that calling non-Jews dogs, reflected the scornful way a Jew at the time of Jesus would look at the non-Jews. Jesus employed this well-known scornful expression of the Jews when he addressed this non-Jewish woman.

Was it all a test of faith given to the woman? Even so, how does one test the faith of the other? Certainly not by calling the other names in public!

Jesus would not test the faith of any Jew before curing him/her. Never once he gave as cruel a test as the one mentioned here: Calling the Canaanite woman a dog in public!

"O woman, great is your faith!" is Jesus' exclamation, evoked by the woman's enduring faith despite his snubbing her. The social prejudices that one grows with do require a few shocks to shake one out of them. Only such experiences as the one we see here, could challenge one's world-view that divided people into the believing Jewish race and a non-believing non-Jewish race. Before calling the woman a dog, Jesus did affirm his prejudice by stating that he came only for the lost sheep of Israel and not to redeem the whole world.

This experience could be seen against the backdrop of an experience of a social worker:

> A social worker, who had just settled in a village in India was playing games with some children of the locality. A young mother, in tears, approached him and said:
> "Sir, please allow my child also to join the game."
> "Of course, he is welcome. Ask him to join straight away."
> "No, sir, it seems, you told him to go away and he is crying at home!"
> "No, I never wanted to exclude anyone. Why should I?"
> "Sir, it seems, you told the children not wearing any clothes to go home and come dressed. . . I have not got any dress made for my son yet. But soon I will get him one. Until then, please allow him to play."

Though the young social worker had come all the way to the village, precisely because of his option for the poor, the very meaning of the word "poor" was to be thrust on him in an encounter like this, long after he had made his option for the poor.

Jesus came to preach faith. But the very depth of faith was thrust on him by the woman considered too low to have faith. Encounters do deepen the perception of the very thing one thinks one knows about.

Definitely, Jesus' life should have been full of such experiences that constantly challenged and shaped his world-view.

Specialty of the Encounter

If this is to be considered a special case, again, the only specialty here is that this is a case of a *non-Jewish untouchable* asking for help.

Let us compare this instance with the way Jesus cured a Jewish untouchable: a leper.

Mt 8:2-3
[2] And there was a leper who came to him and knelt before him, saying, "Lord, if you choose, you can make me clean." [3] He stretched out his hand and touched him, saying, "I do choose. Be made clean!" Immediately his leprosy was cleansed.

Here, Jesus does not have the leper pass any faith-test. It looks as if the leper is testing the love Jesus has for him. Jesus too, expresses his love for the leper with a miraculous cure, without any faith-test.

We saw, earlier, how the reflection of Jesus as a worker had made him interpret the Sabbath law as one made for man. With an experience restricted to his Jewish culture alone, Jesus could not have gone beyond the law and the prophets.

The Canaanite woman and the centurion had faith without the aid of the law and the prophets. Their faith shook Jesus and made him see the relative unimportance of the law and the prophets for one to have deep faith. Besides, instead of helping Jews to grow in faith, the Mosaic Law had only made them feel superior to others and oblivious of their deep faith life. After his encounter with the Canaanite woman and the centurion, Jesus could easily liberate himself from the Mosaic Law. Jesus had a revolutionary change in his understanding of the faith of people around him. Faith was open to one and all; not to Jews alone.

An Untouchable and the Model of the new Law

Jesus eventually went far beyond his original prejudices and put a Samaritan as a model for all who aspire to reach eternal life.

This is seen from the story told by Jesus about a Samaritan.

Lk 10:29-37

[29] But wanting to justify himself, he asked Jesus, "And who is my neighbor?" [30] Jesus replied, "A man was going down from Jerusalem to Jericho, and fell into the hands of robbers, who stripped him, beat him, and went away, leaving him half dead. [31] Now by chance a priest was going down that road; and when he saw him, he passed by on the other side. [32] So likewise a Levite, when he came to the place and saw him, passed by on the other side. [33] But a Samaritan while traveling came near him; and when he saw him, he was moved with pity. [34] He went to him and bandaged his wounds, having poured oil and wine on them. Then he put him on his own animal, brought him to an inn, and took care of him. [35] The next day he took out two denarii, gave them to the innkeeper, and said, 'Take care of him; and when I come back, I will repay you whatever more you spend.' [36] Which of these three, do you think, was a neighbor to the man who fell into the hands of the robbers?" [37] He said, "The one who showed him mercy." Jesus said to him, "Go and do likewise."

Jesus told this story as an answer to the question put forth by a lawyer as to what one must do to inherit eternal life. Jesus starts the reply with a counter question:

Lk: 10:26

He said to him, "What is written in the law? What do you read there?"

Jesus talks about the law, but with a qualification as to how it is read. He appreciates the lawyer who has read it in a way integrating love of God with love of neighbor.

Jesus' Priority Changes

Further, as a reply to the second question regarding who a neighbor is, Jesus makes his views/options very explicit as he chooses neither the priest nor the Levite but a Samaritan as the one whose footsteps anyone desirous of eternal life should follow.

The world is full of broken people lying by the way side. And it is too risky to go to their rescue. Yet, Jesus dare say that loving a wounded neighbor, which the priest found distracting from his journey to Jerusalem, is the way to fulfil the law!

To the Jews, faith seemed to be the product of reading the Scriptures, worship in the temple and pious living. Yet, the Jewish culture that was full of all these, could not produce the faith of a centurion or that of a Canaanite woman!

Jesus, therefore, caricatures the priest and the Levite, in his parable, to show the futility of religious practices. In Jesus' view, the journey to the temple does not take one to God. But straying from the way to the temple, in the interest of one's wounded neighbor, does. This is a 'secular' answer that Jesus gives to the eternally 'religious' question. And we could say for certain that Jesus could not have got it from his Jewish cultural background alone.

Love, according to Jesus, is not a commandment to be fulfilled. Love is just loving. Loving a neighbor, the least of one's neighbors, is loving God. For God is Love. Therefore, Jesus proposes giving food, clothing, shelter and freedom to those who are denied of them to be the only condition to those aspiring to join the company of God.

Proposing love as the corner stone of one's faith life, Jesus has come a long way, from a narrow view of the world defined by the law books of the Bible. This liberation from the clutches of the rigid law demolishes all barriers created by it - even the barriers between races. And, that Jesus totally got out of his racial prejudices is seen, when, in the parable of the Good Samaritan, he quite mischievously makes fun of the practice of untouchability.

Jesus the Mischievous

In his story addressed to a 'touchable' Jewish audience, an untouchable helps the Jew. The details he paints, as an expert in telling stories, hit hard on the sensibilities of the proud Jews. Let us analyze:

The Samaritan came to where the Jew was! (And the Jew did not run away for fear of pollution; he was wounded, and let's excuse him!)

He bound up his wounds! (How does it feel to get one's wounds bound by an untouchable? With his untouchable clothes and with his untouchable hands? Oh, that's only a medical aid!)

He poured oil and wine! (Is it all right to allow the untouchable's oil and wine to be applied? Perhaps only as medicine?!)

He set him on his own beast! (If the Samaritan's touch could pollute, what about the touch of his donkey? Maybe, that's only an ambulance!)

He brought him to an inn and took care of him! (A Jew being personally nursed by an untouchable for one full day? Necessity knows no laws, does it?)

Next day, the untouchable's money is used to foot the bill! (Anyway the money was touched by the innkeeper only!)

It's not all over; he goes with a command and a promise to the innkeeper: "Take care of him"; "I will repay" (A Jew under the sustained care of a Samaritan. That's too much!)

Jesus must have enjoyed himself telling the story and watching the faces of the 'touchables' turning sour with each mention of the untouchable's act of love!

Jesus has come a long way from calling an untouchable a dog to making an untouchable the ideal person to be followed. "Go and do likewise!" Go and do like a Samaritan would do to a wounded man by the way side. Go and love your wounded neighbor as a Samaritan, would do!

Jesus has taken the listeners' attention to a deeper level. In Jesus's view, love of neighbor is not loving someone living in the neighboring building. It is loving the one lying on the wayside robbed of his dignity. Who would love the wounded neighbor? And his answer is that it is the untouchable, the least and the last person in the social hierarchy.

What is so special about the love of the Samaritans? Of the untouchables? It is that the untouchables contribute to society by way of their labor, despite being exploited by the society.

Jesus, by placing precisely a Samaritan in the parable, wants to show the greatness of being a Samaritan. Unfortunately, our modem-day religious leaders have called it the parable of A Good Samaritan, showing their unwillingness to accept the goodness of Samaritans as a class.

Jesus was not telling the story of one bad priest versus one Good Samaritan. He was condemning the priestly class and upholding the class considered untouchables. Otherwise, Jesus could have very well told the story as between a good priest who helped and a bad priest who did not help.

Somewhere in the life of Jesus, he should have gone through some wonderful experience of the way the oppressed shared their lives. Otherwise, it would be very difficult to explain his attitudinal change, and that too to such an extent! From the earlier command "Do not be like them", taught by Jesus about non-Jews, to the "Go and do likewise" command of his that refers to a Samaritan, it is a complete reversal!

Of the ten lepers Jesus cured, only the Samaritan came back to thank him for the cure he received. It was a very special experience for Jesus, as he himself expresses:

Lk 17:12-19
[12] As he entered a village, ten lepers approached him. Keeping their distance, [13] they called out, saying, "Jesus, Master, have mercy on us!" [14] When he saw them, he said to them, "Go and show yourselves to the priests." And as they went, they were made clean. [15] Then one of them, when he saw that he was healed, **turned back, praising God with a loud voice. [16] He prostrated himself at Jesus' feet and thanked him. And he was a Samaritan. [17] Then Jesus asked, "Were not ten made clean? But the other nine, where are they? [18] Was none of them found to return and give praise to God except this foreigner?"** [19] Then he said to him, "Get up and go on your way; your faith has made you well."

A Samaritan cared to respond to Jesus' love more than the nine other Jewish lepers. Jesus noted the fact of the one who came back being a foreigner. This encounter with the cured Samaritan leper, opened Jesus' eyes to the fact that love and gratitude are available in abundance rather with the non-Jews than with the Jews.

Untouchables Savior of the Savior!

Probably, when Jesus went underground to avoid being caught to be murdered by the Jewish leaders, he had more of the love and affection of the Samaritans!

Jn 11:53-54
[53] So from that day on they planned to put him to death. [54] Jesus therefore no longer walked about openly among the Jews, but went from there to a town called Ephraim in the region near the wilderness, and he remained there with the

disciples.

Jesus worked for the Jews and directed his disciples, too, to work exclusively for the uplift of the Jews. All his miracle cures and preaching were confined to the Jews. The non-Jews deprived of the favors from his powerful hands, could have felt left out or even insulted by his attitude to them. In this context, they could have had enough reason to betray him to those who sought his life. Yet, as typical of the oppressed anywhere, they supported him in his misery of having to live a fugitive. Non-Jews, (Samaritans?) helped Jesus escape death from his own people.

Thus, Jesus who once rejected the untouchables and was also rejected by them (cf. Lk 9:51ff) could make the untouchables the model for so arranging one's way of life here on earth as to ensure the kingdom of God hereafter.

Little wonder then that he was also labelled by his religious teachers as a Samaritan!

Jn 8:48-49
[48] The Jews answered him, "Are we not right in saying that **you are a Samaritan** and have a demon?" [49] Jesus answered, "I do not have a demon; but I honor my Father, and you dishonor me ..."

Jesus refutes the charge that he was possessed by a demon. But, he does not protest against being called a Samaritan. He must have accepted it as a compliment?

What better compliment could be paid to a teacher, who commanded everyone to live/love like a Samaritan/ Dalit than to be called a Samaritan/ Dalit!

Jesus And Untouchability

4. DISCIPLES OF JESUS AND UNTOUCHABILITY

It is true that the apostles chosen by Jesus were simple people and not very much educated. But one's simplicity and good heartedness alone do not help one to get out of racial prejudices.

Besides, the training Jesus gave them was very short, lasting only three years. Did the disciples learn to accept the non-Jews as much as Jesus did? To find an answer to this question, we will have to see what the apostles did after Jesus left them.

Jewish Identity of Christians

Most Christians believe that Jesus established a well-organized religion and left its management in the hands of his chosen apostles under the leadership of Peter. The events that followed the murder and resurrection of Jesus do not appear to prove these assumptions. The disciples were not even aware that they belonged to a different religion called Christianity. Even the name 'Christians' was a gift from Antioch. It was not given to them by Jesus or the apostles.

Acts 11:25-26
[25] Then Barnabas went to Tarsus to look for Saul, [26] and when he had found him, he brought him to Antioch. So it was that for an entire year they met with the church and taught a great many people, and it was in Antioch that the disciples were first called "Christians."

Christians at the Temple

Where did this 'Church' (the group consisting of the disciples of Jesus) meet for their worship of God?

Acts 2:44-47
[44] All who believed were together and had all things in common; [45] they would sell their possessions and goods and distribute the proceeds to all, as any had need. [46] **Day by day, as they spent much time together in the temple, they broke bread at home** and ate their food with glad and generous hearts, [47] praising God and having the goodwill of all the people ...

Christians spent much time in the Jewish temple. They attended the service that was going on there. As such, no church building had come up.

Why did Christians attend the temple? Did Jesus teach them to do that? Did he take his disciples to attend services there regularly or hold prayer meetings at the temple?

We hardly ever find Jesus in prayer in the temple. Each time he was found in the temple or in any synagogue, there was some trouble or other, much of which was of his own creation. Remember his observation in the temple on the widow's offerings, curing in the synagogue on Sabbath, his sermon in the synagogue of his hometown, etc.

And when Jesus was driving out the merchants and moneychangers from the temple, Jesus was not just doing a cleaning-up operation. His action was against the sacrificial rituals that went on in the temple. Why, then, did the early disciples of Jesus attend temple?

One might think that they went to the temple out of habit but only to pray and not to make ritual sacrifices. This claim is disproved as we have evidence from the Acts to show that even the apostles did make offerings in the temple after Jesus left them.

Even if one should assume that the disciples went to the temple only to pray, why did they hold prayer in the temple at all?

Jesus and the Temple

Jesus indicated a different way altogether for worshipping the Father:

Jn 4:19-24

[19] The woman (Samaritan) said to him, "Sir, I see that you are a prophet. [20] Our ancestors worshipped on this mountain, but you say that the place where people must worship is in Jerusalem." [21] Jesus said to her, "Woman, believe me, the hour is coming when you will worship the Father neither on this mountain nor in Jerusalem." [22] You worship what you do not know; we worship what we know, for salvation is from the Jews. [23] But the hour is coming, and is now here, when **the true worshippers will worship the Father in spirit and truth, for the Father seeks such as these to worship him. [24] God is spirit, and those who worship him must worship in spirit and truth.**"

Jesus explicitly ruled out worship in the temple. By his teaching and personal example, he indicated different sets of locations to one wanting to pray:

Lk 6:12

Now during those days he went out to the **mountain** to pray; and he spent the night in prayer to God.

Mt 26:36

Then Jesus went with them to a **place called Gethsemane**; and he said to his disciples, "Sit here while I go over there and pray."

Mt 6:6

"But whenever you pray, go into **your room** and shut the door and pray to your Father who is in secret; and your Father who sees in secret will reward you."

In spite of such teachings and examples, the very apostle who records the words Jesus addressed to the Samaritan woman's query about the right place of worship, is found going to the temple at the hour of prayer.

Acts 3:1
One day Peter and John were going up to the temple at the hour of prayer, at three O' clock in the afternoon.

What was the first pope of the Christians trying to do at the temple of the Jews? May be, he just went there to pray along with the Christians who attended the temple service. Even then we could still ask: why at all in the temple?

It appears that the early Jewish disciples of Jesus thought of themselves more as Jews than as the followers of Jesus.

Early Disciples Follow the Old Law

This comes through in the words of the elders of the Church at Jerusalem on Paul's visit there:

Acts 21:17-26
[17] When we arrived in Jerusalem, the brothers welcomed us warmly. [18] The next day Paul went with us to visit James; and all the elders were present. [19] After greeting them, he related one by one the things that God had done among the Gentiles through his ministry. [20] When they heard it, they praised God. Then they said to him, **"You see, brother, how many thousands of believers there are among the Jews, and they are all zealous for the law.** [21] They have been told about you that you teach all the Jews living among the Gentiles to forsake Moses, and that you tell them not to circumcise their children or observe the customs. [22] What then is to be done? They will certainly hear that you have come. [23] So do what we tell you. We have four men who are under a vow. [24] **Joining these men, go through the rite of purification with them, and pay for the shaving of their heads. Thus all will know that there is nothing in what they**

64

have been told about you, but that you yourself observe and guard the law. [25] But as for the Gentiles who have become believers, we have sent a letter with our judgement that they should abstain from what has been sacrificed to idols and from blood and from what is strangled and from fornication." [26] **Then Paul took the men, and the next day, having purified himself, he entered the temple with them, making public the completion of the days of purification when the sacrifice would be made for each of them.**

The apostles in Jerusalem had with them Jewish converts who were zealous for the Mosaic Law. They forced Paul to submit to the Mosaic Law.

Paul had found fault with for preaching against circumcision and the Jewish customs. He had to purify himself by observing certain rituals in the Jerusalem temple. Besides, he was asked to foot the bill for his purification and for fulfilling the vows of four others. Paul had polluted himself by not being serious about the Mosaic Law and customs! Therefore, he was judged impure!

Here James is seen trying to appease the Jewish Christians by forcing Paul to submit himself to purificatory rituals. **How far removed the concerns of the Bishop of Jerusalem, James, are from those of Jesus!**

Early Disciples under the Authority of Judaism

The early Christians thought of themselves as part and parcel of Judaism.

Perhaps, it was not the fault of the Christians and their leaders that they got mixed up with another religion different from their own. May be, Jesus had not made himself clear about what he wanted to build on the rock called Peter. For instance, when Jesus cured the leper, as observed in the previous pages, Jesus directed him to go to the temple and do what was commanded of the Mosaic Law! Jesus claimed, too, to have come to fulfil the law.

The effect of such and other teachings of Jesus, added to their Jewish origins, left the followers of Jesus under the authority of the Judaic priests.

When Peter was summoned and thrashed for speaking about Jesus, he would not reply saying, 'If I, the Pope, did not speak of Jesus, who else would?' Nor did he say that, on the principle of non-interference in the matters of other religions, the Jews should keep themselves off from the affairs of his Church. Rather, he submitted to the thrashing:

Acts 4:1-3, 19, 20

[1] While Peter and John were speaking to the people, the priests, the captain of the temple, and the Sadducees came to them, [2] much annoyed because they were teaching the people and proclaiming that in Jesus there is the resurrection of the dead. [3] So they arrested them and put them in custody until the next day, for it was already evening.

[19] But Peter and John answered them, "Whether it is right in the God's sight to listen to you rather than to God, you must judge; [20] for we cannot keep from speaking about what we have seen and heard."

Acts 5:17, 18, 40

[17] Then the high priest took action; he and all who were with him (that is, the sect of the Sadducees), being filled with jealousy, [18] arrested the apostles and put them in the public prison.

[40] And when they had called in the apostles, they had them flogged. Then they ordered them not to speak in the name of Jesus, and let them go.

The apostles responded to the threats from the Jewish

authorities only as any Jewish lay person would. Their faith in Jesus does not appear to have given them an awareness that they belonged to a different religious organization.

Christians: an Erring Sect of Judaism

Also, the Jewish authorities did not tell the early Christians to get away from the temple on their having become Christians. Rather, their stand seems to be one of trying to save these erring sheep of Judaism from the error of believing Jesus to be the Messiah.

> **Acts 5:34-40**
>
> 34 But a Pharisee in the council named Gamaliel, a teacher of the law, respected by all the people, stood up and ordered the men to be put outside for a short time. 35 Then he said to them, "Fellow Israelites, consider carefully what you propose to do to these men. 36 For some time ago Theudas rose up, claiming to be somebody, and a number of men, about four hundred, joined him; but he was killed, and all who followed him were dispersed and disappeared. 37 After him Judas the Galilean rose up at the time of the census and got people to follow him; he also perished, and all who followed him were scattered. 38 So in the present case, I tell you, keep away from these men and let them alone; because if this plan or this undertaking is of human origin, it will fail; 39 but if it is of God, you will not be able to overthrow them - in that case you may even be found fighting against God!" They were convinced by him, 40 and when they had called in the apostles, they had them flogged. Then they ordered them not to speak in the name of Jesus, and let them go.

The acceptance of Gamaliel's advice meant that the followers of Jesus could go on attending the temple. Hence, ***there was no division as yet between the disciples of Jesus and the Jews as people belonging to two separate and distinct religions.***

Non-Jews into the Fold

The disciples of Jesus were all Jews. Even after the murder and resurrection of Jesus, the community of disciples remained faithful to the Judaic religion with its Mosaic laws and temple worship. But the book of Acts bears evidence to show that despite their Jewish origin and identity, this community accepted non-Jews into their fold.

The consciousness of a Jew of himself being purer than the rest of the world leads to the question as to why or how the first disciples of Jesus, allowed the untouchables (non-Jews) into their group.

The Spirit Overtaking the Apostles!

We find that the non-Jews got into the community of disciples not as a result of the principle of equality preached by Jesus. It was as if they were brought in much against the will of the disciples themselves!

It rather seems to be that the Holy Spirit could not be kept under control by the apostles who would have preferred to work among the Jews only. The Spirit blew where it willed and kept falling on one and all, not discriminating on the basis of castes, races and colors, and making disciples of all nations.

> **Acts 10:44-48**
> [44] While Peter was still speaking, the Holy Spirit fell upon all who heard the word. [45] The circumcised believers who had come with Peter were astounded that the gift of the Holy Spirit had been poured out even on the Gentiles, [46] for they heard them speaking in tongues and extolling God. Then Peter said, [47] "Can anyone withhold the water for baptizing these people who have received the Holy Spirit just as we have?" [48] So he ordered them to be baptized in the name of the Jesus Christ. Then they invited him to stay for several days.

The circumcised men, including Peter, were amazed that the

uncircumcised also could receive the Spirit.

The Spirit went ahead and administered the "sacrament of confirmation" on non-Jews, not even waiting for them to be first baptized by the apostles. Rather, Peter had to baptize them, to keep pace with the Spirit.

Baptizing the untouchables must have been a very difficult decision for Peter to make. The very idea of having to go to the house of Cornelius, an untouchable, was revolting to him. He had gone through a bout of nausea at the very thought of having to eat unclean animals. He had to be cajoled by a heavenly voice thrice over before he could decide to visit Cornelius. The heavenly voice had to instruct Peter not to call anything unclean.
Acts 10:14-15
[14] But Peter said, "By no means, Lord; for I have never eaten anything that is profane or unclean." [15] The voice said to him again, a second time, "What God has made clean, you must not call profane."

It was after this heavenly revelation that Peter had no objections to accepting the invitation of Cornelius to visit his house.
Acts 10:27-29
[27] And as he (Peter) talked with him (Cornelius), he went in and found that many had assembled; [28] and he said to them, "You yourselves know that it is unlawful for a Jew to associate with or to visit a Gentile; but God has shown me that I should not call anyone profane or unclean. [29] So when I was sent for, I came without objection. Now may I ask why you sent for me?"
The vision of Peter was about "animals and beasts of prey and reptiles and birds of the air" (Acts 11:5). Yet he dared to say that Goo had shown him that he should not call any man common or unclean. This mixing up of things eaten with the people eating is common to any culture.

Peter Dragged by the Spirit

The Jewish Christians who did not have such visions could not digest the idea of Peter entering the house of untouchables:

Acts 11:2-3

²So when Peter went up to Jerusalem, the circumcised believers criticized him, ³saying, "Why did you go to uncircumcised men and eat with them?"

Peter took a very democratic way of dealing with the problem. Interestingly, his answer betrays his identifying himself with the "circumcision party" totally. Says he:

Acts 11:17

"If then God gave them the same gift that he gave us when we believed in the Lord Jesus Christ, who was I that I could hinder God?"

Note the words 'us' and 'we' Peter uses to refer to Jews in contrast to 'them' to mean non-Jewish Christians. He then pleads helplessness for having done the act of baptizing the untouchables: "Who was I that I could hinder God?"

Not that Peter was comfortable to go to the houses of untouchables and baptize them. He was not able to withhold God who led him there!

The apostles baptized non-Jews not because they were able to see great faith among the non-Jews as Jesus could, nor because they accepted them as equals based on Jesus' teachings, but because the Spirit had fallen on the non-Jews. There is hardly anything positive that the Jewish disciples could find in the non-Jews as reason for their inclusion into the community. Such was their Jewish pride!

A Special Missionary to Non-Jews

It was left to Paul, the one-time persecutor of Christians, who had a vision and got converted to the new Way, to become the greatest apostle of the Gentiles, the Dalits. But, even as regards

Paul, his option for the Dalits did not actually follow his heavenly vision, as a matter of course. **In fact, Paul's going to the non-Jews to preach Jesus appears to be rather out of a sense of frustration at his failure to convert his fellow Jews than in obedience to the Lord:**

Acts 13:44-47

[44] The next Sabbath almost the whole city gathered to hear the word of the Lord. [45] But when the Jews saw the crowds, they were filled with jealousy; and blaspheming, they contradicted what was spoken by Paul!' [46] Then both Paul and Barnabas spoke out boldly, saying, "It was necessary that the word of God should be spoken first to you. Since you reject it and judge yourselves to be unworthy of eternal life, we are now turning to the Gentiles. [47] For so the Lord has commanded us...

Way back during the conversion episode, Ananias was informed by the Lord:

Acts 9:15-16

[15] But the Lord said to him (Ananias), "Go, for he (Paul) is an instrument whom I have chosen to bring my name before Gentiles and kings and before the people of Israel; [16] I myself will show him how much he must suffer for the sake of my name."

Perhaps Ananias did not communicate the news to Paul about his being chosen for Gentile missions. Or maybe, Paul's Jewish faith that put Jews first, prevented him from understanding the mission given him for the Gentiles. But, when Paul did make the choice of turning to the Gentiles, his mission infuriated the Jews. There were even attempts on his life...

Acts 14:19

[19] But Jews came there from Antioch and Iconium and won over the crowds. Then they stoned Paul and dragged him out of the city, supposing that he was dead.

Handling the Uncircumcised – a Problem

While the non-Christian Jews were getting concerned about the Christian faith that Paul was spreading, the Christian Jews, too, had reasons to be worried about the missions of Paul among the untouchables. **Paul preached that one could become a Christian without undergoing circumcision, that is, without becoming a Jew, without having to change one's caste.**

Acts 15:1-2
[1] Then certain individuals came down from Judea and were teaching the brothers, "Unless you are circumcised according to the custom of Moses, you cannot be saved." [2] And after Paul and Barnabas had no small dissension and debate with them, Paul and Barnabas and some of the others were appointed to go up to Jerusalem to discuss this question with the apostles and the elders.

In plain terms, the question meant: why not convert an untouchable first to Judaism and thereby purify him (make him belong to the pure Jewish race) before converting him to Christianity?

According to the Hindu belief, each person, on dying, assumes one of the various forms of life that is available on earth, in a never ending cycle of birth and rebirth. The status of the new form that one assumes in the next birth, would depend on the merits one acquired during the present life. The more the merit, the higher the form of life. The one with a very low deposit of merit may be born even as an animal and the one with a very high amount of it could be born into a high caste, even as a Brahmin.

The Brahmin authors of the Sutra (Rules of life) promised salvation to the Shudra (untouchable) only through the intermediacy of birth in higher castes. In plain words, it was tantamount to asking him to wait till doomsday.

What cannot be cured has to be endured. Once an untouchable, an untouchable till death. That is the Indian context.

Whereas, a Gentile could become a Jew, i.e., a low caste person could become an upper caste person by circumcision. That was the context of the early Christians.

Naturally, the Jewish Christians demanded non-Jewish converts first to become clean by embracing Judaism and then to enter Christianity.

Acts 15:4-5
[4] When they came to Jerusalem, they were welcomed by the church and the apostles and the elders, and they reported all that God had done with them. [5] But some believers who belonged to the sect of the Pharisees stood up and said, "It is necessary for them to be circumcised and ordered to keep the law of Moses."

There were Christians who could be grouped as the 'sect of the Pharisees' based on their commitment to the Mosaic Law. They demanded a strict adherence to the law. One could imagine their pharisaic superiority hindering the admission of the untouchables into the community.

The first pope had to tell them that baptism cleans the untouchables:

Acts 15:6-11
[6] The apostles and the elders met together to consider this matter. [7] After there had been much debate, Peter stood up and said to them, "My brothers, you know that in the early days God made a choice among you, that I should be the one through whom the Gentiles would hear the message of the good news and become believers. [8] And God, who knows the human heart, testified to them by giving them the Holy Spirit, just as he did to us; [9] and in cleansing their hearts by faith he has made no distinction between them and us. [10] Now therefore why are you putting God to the test by placing on the neck of the disciples a yoke that neither our ancestors nor we have been able to bear? [11] On the contrary, we believe that we will be saved through the grace of the Lord Jesus, just as they will."

The problem of 'they' being unclean is solved by their faith. God 'cleansed' their hearts with faith.

Faith is almost as good as circumcision in its capacity to make one clean: faith cleanses the hearts of the faithful. Hence, there is no need for circumcision of the uncircumcised believers. Peter could only assure the Jewish Christians that the 'hearts' (souls?) of the uncircumcised were cleaned by their faith. How were their bodies to be made clean without circumcision and Mosaic Law?

Hence, certain provisions from the Mosaic Law were imposed on non-Jewish Christians to make them clean. It was new wine poured into old skins!

New One in Old Skin

> **Acts 15:13, 19-21, 23, 28-29**
> [13] After they finished speaking, James replied...
> [19] Therefore I have reached the decision that we should not trouble those Gentiles who are turning to God, [20] but we should write to them to abstain only from things polluted by idols and from fornication and from whatever has been strangled and from blood. [21] For in every city, for generations past, Moses has had those who proclaim him, for he has been read aloud every Sabbath in the synagogues."
> . . . [23] with the following letter: "The brothers, both the apostles and the elders, to the believers of Gentile origin in Antioch and Syria and Cilicia, greetings.
> [28] For it has seemed good to the Holy Spirit and to us to impose on you no further burden than these essentials: [29] that you abstain from what has been sacrificed to idols and from blood and from what is strangled and from fornication. If you keep yourselves from these, you will do well. Farewell."

The Judgement delivered by James imposes the burden of observing a set of 'these essentials' on non-Jewish followers of Jesus as a means to avoid pollutions.

> **Act 15:20**
> But we should write to them to abstain only from things polluted by idols and from fornication and from whatever has been strangled and from blood.

The best part of this decision was that, by deciding against forcing the non-Jewish converts to get circumcised, it left the non-Jews free from the burden of embracing Judaism. It opened the doors of the Church to the non-Jews.

The worst part of it was the imposing of certain Jewish customs on non-Jewish converts on the ground of avoiding pollutions. Implicit in this imposition is an air of superiority of the Jewish race as one being purer than others!

The laws deliberately broken by Jesus to abolish this division of people into pure and impure were thus brought into the Church by the backdoor, 'avoiding pollution' being a justification.

The decision was in effect a compromise on the very principle of equality preached by Jesus. It dictated against the freedom and dignity of the non-Jews in the nascent Church.

And this old wine poured into new skin made the skin burst, resulting in the fall of the first pope.

The fall of the First Pope

Peter respected the judgement James delivered at the Jerusalem Council. He related with non-Jewish Christians without any show of racial superiority when he visited the Church at Antioch. Yet, when some of James' relatives came to Antioch, Peter could not continue relating to the non-Jewish Christians as equals. He withdrew and the other Jewish Christians followed suit, including

Paul's cherished companion Barnabas.

Gal 2:11-14

[11] But when Cephas came to Antioch, I opposed him to his face, because he stood self-condemned; [12] for until certain people came from James, he used to eat with the Gentiles. But after they came, he drew back and kept himself separate for fear of the circumcision faction. [13] And the other Jews joined him in this hypocrisy, so that even Barnabas was led astray by their hypocrisy. [14] But when I saw that they were not acting consistently with the truth of the gospel, I said to Cephas before them all, "If you, though a Jew, live like a Gentile and not like a Jew, how can you compel the Gentiles to live like Jews?"

Peter was afraid of the presence of the 'circumcision party' who were coming from James. It is good to remember that it was James who delivered the judgement against the demands of the party of Pharisees and ruled out the imposition of circumcision on non-Jewish Christians.

James must have made a volte-face. Or else, there is no meaning in Peter fearing James' men. Perhaps, James who delivered the judgement was so dishonest as not to allow his own judgment to be implemented against the interest of his clan?

Paul sounds very sarcastic when he calls James' men the circumcision party coming from James.

Paul is not just making some careless statements here. He is very angry with the apostles at Jerusalem. Just a few verses preceding the one we are considering now, he talks about them:

Gal 2:6, 9, 11

[6] And from those (James, Cephas and John) 'who were supposed to be acknowledged leaders (what they actually were makes no difference to me; God shows no partiality) - those leaders contributed nothing to me.

[9] and when James and Cephas and John, who were

acknowledged pillars, recognized the grace that had been given to me, they gave to Barnabas and me the right hand of fellowship, agreeing that we should go to the Gentiles and they to the circumcised.
[11] But when Cephas came to Antioch, I opposed him to his face, because he stood self-condemned . . .

Obviously something is wrong. Peter's boycotting of meals with non-Jewish people was, thought Paul, contrary to the teachings of the gospels. Paul could dare say that Peter stood condemned.

Paul could not think of a worse crime a pope could commit than the one of discriminating against a people on the ground of untouchability. Hence he 'opposed Peter to his face' 'before them all'. The 'hypocrisy' of Peter deserved no private admonition. It called for a public condemnation.

Paul's question posed to Peter is even more sarcastic. According to Paul, if Peter believed that eating with non-Jewish Christians polluted a Jew, then Peter had already made himself a polluted person by having eaten with the non-Jews prior to the arrival of James' men. A polluted Peter had then lost his moral rights to ask the non-Jewish people to live like the Jews! Peter is paid back in his own coin by Paul in the argument: "If you, though a Jew, live like a Gentile and not like a Jew, how can you compel Gentiles to live like the Jews?

Christ's Death Laid Waste

Paul understood the death of Jesus in terms of the struggle Jesus put up against the law that distinguished people as pure and polluting. Hence Paul could say:
Gal 2:21
... If justification comes through the law, then Christ died for nothing.

How sad that Peter had not understood the truth of the gospels and had been insincere to the agreement entered into at Jerusalem! This pharisaic party of disciples that had got encouragement from the pillars at Jerusalem bewitched the Galatians to accepting circumcision. From Paul's letter to the Galatians, it looks like the Galatians were ready to get circumcised, if not already circumcised. Paul condemns those Galatians:

Gal 3:1-3

[1]You foolish Galatians! Who has bewitched you? It was before your eyes that Jesus Christ was publicly exhibited as crucified! [2]The only thing I want to learn from you is this: Did you receive the Spirit by doing the works of the law or by believing what you heard? [3]Are you so foolish? Having started with the Spirit, are you now ending with the flesh?

Pauline Theology of Dalit Christian Liberation

Paul maintained that the **practice of untouchability goes against the truth of the gospels.** He went on to explain the truth of the gospels in contrast to the falsehood of the Mosaic Law.

Mosaic Law divided people into pure Jews and impure non-Jews (Greeks); into the pure free persons and the dirty slaves; into pure males and impure females. But, in Jesus, all these divisions disappeared.

Gal 3:28

There is no longer Jew or Greek, there is no longer slave or free, there is no longer male and female; for all of you are one in Christ Jesus.

Rom 10:12-13

[12] For there is no distinction between Jew and Greek; the same Lord is Lord of all and is generous to all who call on him. [13] For, "Everyone who calls on the name of the Lord shall be saved."

Peter and his companions at Jerusalem seemed to rely on the

Mosaic Law. Paul had serious reservations or even objections to their stand:

Gal 3:10-12, 14

[10] For all who rely on the works of the law are under a curse; for it is written, "Cursed is everyone who does not observe and obey all the things written in the book of the law." [11] Now it is evident that no one is justified before God by the law; for "The one who is righteous will live by faith." [12] But the law does not rest on faith; on the contrary, "Whoever does the works of the law will live by them."

[14] in order that in Christ Jesus the blessing of Abraham might come to the Gentiles, so that we might receive the promise of the Spirit through faith.

If circumcision was very much needed for one to be saved, as believed by the party of the Pharisees in Jerusalem, how was Abraham saved? Was Abraham purified by circumcision before God came to save him? No. Abraham had faith in God and he was saved. The circumcision that followed was only a symbol of his having been saved. The symbol cannot save. It is the Spirit that saves through faith.

Thus, if Abraham was saved when he was not circumcised, that is, when he was still a non-Jew, why should non-Jews be compelled to become Jews to be saved? Is not their faith in Jesus enough?

Faith versus Law

Where did the Jewish race originate from? From the Law of Moses or from the faith of Abraham? That is the way Paul poses the question and finds the faith of Abraham to be the basis for the Jewish race.

Gal 3:6-9, 17-18

[6] Just as Abraham "believed God, and it was reckoned to him as righteousness," [7] so, you see, those who believe are the descendants of Abraham. [8] And the scripture, foreseeing

that God would justify the Gentiles by faith, declared the Gospel beforehand to Abraham, saying, "All the Gentiles shall be blessed in you." [9] For this reason, those who believe are blessed with Abraham who believed.

[17] My point is this: the law, which came four hundred thirty years later, does not annul a covenant previously ratified by God, so as to nullify the promise. [18]For if the inheritance comes from the law, it no longer comes from the promise; but God granted it to Abraham through the promise.

In Paul's view, then, faith saves the believer as much as it saved Abraham. Paul takes pains to calculate and show that the law, dear to the Jews, came 430 years after Abraham. Were not Jews existing as Jews before this law came in? Or is Abraham to be considered a gentile for his not having come under the Law of Moses?

The Gentiles become children of Abraham through sharing in the same faith, and, therefore, they all become Jews by faith. There is no need to follow the law to make one a Jew, a child of Abraham.

Gal 3:23-29

[23] Now before faith came, we were imprisoned and guarded under the law until faith would be revealed. [24] Therefore the law was our disciplinarian until Christ came, so that we might be justified by faith. [25] But now that faith has come, we are no longer subject to a disciplinarian, [26] for in Christ Jesus you are all children of God through faith. [27] As many of you as were baptized into Christ have clothed yourselves with Christ. [28] There is no longer Jew or Greek, there is no longer slave or free, there is no longer male and female; for all of you are one in Christ Jesus. [29] And if you belong to Christ, then you are Abraham's offspring, heirs according to the promise.

Why do People Insist on Circumcision

People coming from Jerusalem, who insisted on circumcision, seemed to have a different motivation for the stand they took:

Gal 4:24-26

²⁴ Now this is an allegory: these women are two covenants. One woman, in fact, is Hagar, from Mount Sinai, bearing children for slavery. ²⁵Now Hagar is Mount Sinai in Arabia and corresponds to the present Jerusalem, for she is in slavery with her children. ²⁶But the other woman corresponds to the Jerusalem above; she is free, and she is our mother.

Thus, those who advocate circumcision are children of slaves. Those who put their trust in faith in Jesus are children of heavenly Jerusalem, argues Paul. Paul attributes motives to their advocacy of circumcision and Mosaic Law. He thinks that they are afraid of being persecuted by the non-converted Jews. They want to avoid the pain of crucifixion at the hands of the Jewish authorities who were becoming less tolerant to the Christians for their association with the untouchables.

Gal 5:11

But my friends, why am I still being persecuted if I am still preaching circumcision? In that case the offense of the cross has been removed.

That is why he could call their fervor for law a hypocrisy: To save their skins they want the foreskin of their fellow Christians.

Gal 5:12

I wish those who unsettle you would castrate themselves!

It is like saying: let those frustrated at not being able to get at your foreskins go and cut off their whole organ ['mutilate themselves' - R.S.V].

Paul analyses the effect of circumcision and finds that it does not confer anything on the person undergoing it. The only effect is that it exposes the flesh!

Gal 6:11-13

[11] See what large letters I make when I am writing in my own hand! [12] It is those who want to make a good showing in the flesh that try to compel you to be circumcised - only that they may not be persecuted for the cross of Christ. [13] Even the circumcised do not themselves obey the law but they want you to be circumcised so that they may boast about your flesh.

To Paul, the champion of the untouchables, every occasion is appropriate to stress the importance of not submitting to circumcision. Talking about the qualities of a good bishop, he says:

Titus 1:9-10, 11, 14-15
[9] He must have a firm grasp of the word that is trustworthy in accordance with the teaching, so that he may be able both to preach with sound doctrine and to refute those who contradict it. [10] There are also many rebellious people, idle talkers and deceivers, especially those of the circumcision; [11] they must be silenced...
[14] not paying attention to Jewish myths or to commandments of those who reject the truth. [15] **To the pure all things are pure, but to the corrupt and unbelieving nothing is pure.**

Paul thinks it to be the important duty of a bishop to silence the circumcision party because they are impure and see everywhere and in everyone impurity. Had they been pure, all things would have been pure for them.

Paul would have every bishop realize that to the pure all things are pure. And they must beware of people who would like to go back to the Mosaic Law. There can be no adherence to a law that leads to distinctions between people and races.

Exception to Paul's Stand on Purity/Pollution

The exception to his stand proves Paul's commitment to the

Spirit of the law:

When it comes to the day-to-day living in mixed groups, there is a need for compromise between people. One needs to follow the policy of cooperation for the sake of peace. While at table with others, courtesy demands that one avoids food repulsive to the neighbor. Writing to the Romans, he would say:

Rom 14:14
[14] I know and am persuaded in the Lord Jesus that nothing is unclean in itself; but it is unclean for anyone who thinks it unclean.

As a code of conduct in a mixed congregation, he would insist on the policy of compromise.

Rom 14:17, 19-21
[17] For the kingdom of God is not food and drink but righteousness and peace and joy in the Holy Spirit.
[19] Let us then pursue what makes for peace and for mutual upbringing. [20] Do not, for the sake of food, destroy the work of God. Everything is indeed clean, but it is wrong for you to make others fall by what you eat; [21] it is good not to eat meat or drink wine or do anything that makes your brother or sister stumble.

One cannot insist on food as a matter of right, when it interferes with the unity among the followers of Jesus. The Kingdom of God does not mean food and drink. If food offered to idols should cause nausea to some, better avoid it for the sake of peace.

Rom 14:1-3
[1] Welcome those who are weak in faith, but not for the purpose of quarreling over opinions. [2] Some believe in eating anything, while the weak eat only vegetables. [3] Those who eat must not despise those who abstain and those abstain must not pass judgment on those who eat: for God has welcomed them.

That is, one gives up an item of food not because it makes him impure and untouchable but because the one around is weak. The weak man eats only vegetables because he fears the meat sold has been polluted by its having been offered to idols.

Paul Rejects Jerusalem Council's Decisions

Paul has obviously explained the conditions laid on the non-Jews at the Jerusalem council in a very different spirit. The Jerusalem council wanted non-Jews to avoid meat offered to idols since it was considered polluting.

1 Cor 8:4, 7-13

[4]Hence, as to the eating of food offered to idols, we know that "no idol in the world really exists," and that "there is no God but one."

[7]It is not everyone, however, who has this knowledge. Since some have become so accustomed to idols until now, they still think of the food they eat as food offered to an idol; and their conscience, being weak, is defiled. [8]"Food will not bring us close to God." We are no worse off if we do not eat, and no better off if we do. [9]But take care that this liberty of yours does not somehow become a stumbling block to the weak. [10]For if others see you, who possess knowledge, eating in the temple of an idol, might they not, since their conscience is weak, be encouraged to the point of eating food sacrificed to idols? [11]So by your knowledge those weak believers for whom Christ died are destroyed. [12]But when you thus sin against members of your family, and wound their conscience when it is weak, you sin against Christ. [13]Therefore, if food is a cause of their falling, I will never eat meat, so that I may not cause one of them to fall.

In Corinth, even meat sold in the market was often what had been offered to idols. And, ordinarily, feasts were held in the temple. What was one to do in such a situation?

Paul does not quote the Jerusalem council's decision and tell the non-Jewish Christians to stop eating meat. He says that meat does not become polluting on being offered to idols. Idols don't exist and, hence, a non-existing thing cannot pollute one's food. Therefore, for that matter, eating in the temple, as it could happen for Christians in Corinth, too, does not make any difference to one who knows that idols do not exist.

Paul had to deal with three types of Christians in this problem of eating meat offered to idols:

The first, the believing non-Jewish Christians who could digest any food as he/she knew that idols did not exist.

The second, the Jewish Christians whose faith was weak as he/she believed in the existence of idol-Gods and, therefore, could not eat what was offered to them.

The third, the new non-Jewish convert who slipped back into his/her old belief system by attending temple festivals forgetting his/her conversion.

The last two categories of people are weaklings. Paul is concerned with them and advises the non-Jewish Christian, who is strong, to be concerned about the weaklings.

Paul gives a positive self-image to the non-Jewish Christians whom he asks to abstain from meat, though the opposite kind of self-image was offered to them by the Jerusalem Council. Paul proves the apostles and disciples at Jerusalem to be weak and ignorant compared to his strong Dalit Christians! If these ignorant people at Jerusalem, i.e., apostles and disciples should keep passing judgement on the knowledgeable non-Jews, then Paul would take a stand against the Jewish Christians:

Col 2:16-23

[16]Therefore do not let anyone condemn you in matters of food and drink or of observing festivals, new moons, or Sabbaths. [17]These are only a shadow of what is to come, but the substance belongs to Christ. [18]Do not let anyone

disqualify you, insisting on self-abasement and worship of angels, dwelling on visions, puffed up without cause by a human way of thinking, [19]and not holding fast to the head, from whom the whole body, nourished and held together through by its ligaments and sinews, grows with a growth that is from God.

[20]If with Christ you died to the elemental spirits of the universe, why do you live as if you still belonged to the world? Why do you submit to regulations, [21]"Do not handle, do not taste, and do not touch"'? [22]All these regulations refer to things that perish with use: they are simply human commands and teachings. [23]These have indeed an appearance of wisdom in promoting self-imposed piety, humility, and severe treatment of the body, but they are of no value in checking self-indulgence.

Yes, to Paul, the teachings of the Jerusalem council have only the 'appearance of wisdom'. They are only 'human precepts and doctrines'. They may be waived and need not be submitted to if they should imply any disqualification.

There cannot be two standards in the matter of morality: one for Jews and another for Greeks. All are equal.

Col 3:5, 8,9,11

[5]Put to death, therefore, whatever in you is earthly: fornication, impurity, passion, evil desire, and greed (which is idolatry).

[8]But now you must get rid of all such things - anger, wrath, malice, slander, and abusive language from your mouth. [9]Do not lie to one another, seeing that you have stripped off the old self with its practices.

[11]In that renewal there is no longer Greek and Jew, circumcised and uncircumcised, barbarian, Scythian, slave and free; but Christ is all and in all!

Paul: a Stout Champion of Untouchable Christians

Paul never gets tired of defending the untouchable Christians. He warns them to beware of those who mutilate the flesh who are after their foreskins, whom he even calls 'dogs'! '

Phil 3:1-5

[1]... To write the same things to you is not troublesome to me, and for you it is a safeguard.

[2]Beware of the dogs, beware of the evil-workers, beware of those who mutilate the flesh! [3]For it is we who are the circumcision, who worship in the Spirit of God and boast in Christ Jesus and have no confidence in the flesh - [4] even though I, too, have reason for confidence in the flesh.

If anyone else has reason to be confident in the flesh, I have more: [5] circumcised on the eighth day, a member of the people of Israel, of the tribe of Benjamin, a Hebrew born of Hebrews; as to the law, a Pharisee...

The prejudice Jesus betrayed against the untouchable woman when he called her clan 'dogs' has gone one full round with Paul calling the Jewish Christian believers 'dogs'. He has also understood that Christians should worship God in spirit and truth. No more are Christians to have anything to do with Judaism that discriminates between the pure and the impure.

Abolition of Untouchability = Birth of Christianity

Had Paul not struggled against the imposition of circumcision and Mosaic Law, all the early Gentile Christians would have first entered Judaism just to become Christians!

The Jewish religious leaders, we saw, waited for the enthusiasm of the followers of Jesus to cool down. They could not find fault with these followers of Jesus on any other count than that they were being misled by the philosophy of Jesus. They were ready to wait and see if the influence of Jesus on these followers would eventually die away. Since the Jewish authorities were ready to wait, there was no need for the disciples of Jesus to think of a separate Church in Jerusalem.

When and why did the followers of Jesus get away from the religion of their origin and establish an identity for themselves as people belonging to a different religion?

We saw Paul stating:

Gal 5:11
But my friends, why am I still being persecuted, if I am still preaching circumcision?

Gal 6:11-12
[11] See what large letters I make when I am writing in my own hand! [12] It is those who want to make a good showing in the flesh that try to compel you to be circumcised - only **that they may not be persecuted** for the cross of Christ.

Paul almost got killed inside the temple when he went in to offer sacrifices because he had been found associating with non-Jews in the city. People thought that he had taken his polluting non-Jewish friends into the temple.

Acts 21:27-31
[27] When the seven days were almost completed, the Jews from Asia, who had seen him in the temple, stirred up the whole crowd. They seized him, [28] shouting, "Fellow Israelites, help! This is the man who is teaching everyone everywhere against our people, our law and this place; more than that, **he has actually brought Greeks into the temple and has defiled this Holy place.**" [29] For they had previously seen Trophimus the Ephesian with him in the city, and they supposed that Paul had brought him into the temple. [30] Then all the city was aroused, and the people rushed together. **They seized Paul and dragged him out of the temple, and immediately the doors were shut.** [31] While they were trying to kill him, word came to the tribunal of the cohort that all Jerusalem was in an uproar.

Christians Thrown out of the Temple

The Jewish Christians had trouble in using the temple and synagogues not because they followed Jesus but because they associated with the polluting castes. To Jews, following Jesus was not as polluting as associating with the non-Jews. The latter polluted them and their holy places. Pollution to themselves and to the temple was too much for the Jews to bear.

Historians tell us that the Jews threw the Christians out of the temple and the synagogues for the simple reason that Christians were polluted by their association with non-Jews. The Jews had to throwaway Christians to keep themselves and their holy places from getting polluted.

It was a difficult task to accomplish: to identify the Jewish followers of Jesus from the rest of the Jews and to throw them out. How did they identify whether the one standing next to them in the synagogue and singing psalms was a follower of Jesus or not?

The Jewish authorities solved it by adding a special curse on Jesus and his followers into the invocations to be recited aloud by the congregation during liturgy. All those tight lipped were identified as Christians and physically thrown out.

The words the Jews had to invoke aloud were:
> **'May the Nazarenes and the heretics be suddenly destroyed and removed from the Book of life.'[8]**

The followers of Jesus were thus thrown out with a stigma struck on their face: impure people!

Christians got their separated identity as members of a new religion when they got thrown out of the temple and the synagogues by force!

---

[8] Henry Chadwick, 'The Early Church', Penguin Books Ltd, England, 1978 ed. p.22

Christians Retort

The way the early Christians reacted to the Jews shows how much they were hurt when the Jews called them a polluting people. They reacted by calling into question the purity of the Jewish race itself! In this background it makes sense that Matthew at the very start of his good news would ridicule the history of the Jews in his genealogy of Jesus.

Mt 1:2, 3, 5, 6
2 **Abraham** was the father of Isaac, and Isaac the father of Jacob...
3 and Judah the father of Perez and Zarah by **Tamar**...
5 and Salmon the father of Boaz, by **Rahab**, and Boaz was the father of Obed by **Ruth**...
6 and Jesse the father of King David.
And David was the father of Solomon by the **wife of Uriah**...

Abraham being the grandfather of Jacob after whom the Jews were called Israelites is mentioned first. If Israelites are children of Jacob, who is a grandson of a non-Jewish Abraham, can't the followers of Jesus be as good as such Jews? In keeping with the tradition of the Jews, Matthew limits himself to using the name of the male parents only while giving the genealogy of Jesus. Yet on four occasions, he takes pains to give the name of the female parent. The only thing that all these four had in common was that they were all non-Jews! Perhaps, the Jews would prefer to erase some of those names from their history.

The book of Genesis tells us, (chapter 38) that Tamar a widow seduced her father-In-law by playing the role of a prostitute. Through this father-in-law she gave birth to an ancestor of their great kings David and Solomon.

Rahab, another ancestral parent of David and Solomon, was not only a non-Jew but a prostitute by profession and it was also through her that the genealogy of David and Solomon continued!

(cf. Jos2.) Ruth was a respectable person, but a foreigner all the same.

How was Solomon the great king born? David got his son Solomon through the wife of another man who was not a Jew but a Hittite. Are not the psalms, sung in the temple from which the followers of Jesus stand excluded, written by this David? If mingling with non-Jews is reason enough to throw one out of the temple, then David should have been thrown out first along with his psalms! How come Solomon born of mixed blood built the temple?

By referring to Tamar, Rahab, Ruth and Bathsheba, Matthew tells the Jews that if the followers of Jesus should be called impure the Jews were no better off. He proves that there is no point in making such distinctions if one is ready to look into one's own history. He even dares to place Mary, the mother of Jesus, as the fifth woman in his genealogy.

The followers of Jesus got a separate identity since they defied the Jewish restrictions on mixing with non-Jews.

A struggle for the annihilation of castes gave birth to the Church!

Jesus And Untouchability

5. THE EARLIEST FOLLOWERS OF JESUS AND THE MISSION OF JESUS

We saw how the followers of Jesus got a separate identity since they defied the Jewish restrictions on mixing with non-Jews, and that *struggle to annihilate untouchability gave birth to the Church.*

That does not in any way mean that Jesus did not built the church. Rather, the Church emerged since *his disciples continued his struggle to abolish all discriminations which was the Spirit of Jesus.* The Spirit that moved them to abandon circumcision and to embrace non-Jews into their fold established the Church.

Since the Church came into existence decades *after* Jesus was murdered on the cross, the gospels that narrate Jesus' life has very little to speak of the Church. In fact, gospels don't use the word "Church" except on *two* occasions. And, both the references are found in Matthew's Gospel only.

The first is when Jesus says to Peter "And I tell you, you are Peter, and on this rock I will build my church..." (Mat 16:18). Jesus does not indicate how specifically or when he'll build his dream; he does not reveal an organizational model on which he will design it.

Surprisingly, when Jesus used the word Church, no one – not even Peter – asked him what he meant by the word Church; they were only worshiping Yahweh in the Temple, or in synagogues; and this word "Church" had not come into existence till much after Jesus died on the cross.

And the other time the word 'church' is used is in the context of Jesus teaching how to settle disputes among the members of the Church:

Mt 18: 15-17

[15] "If another member of the **church** sins against you, go and point out the fault when the two of you are alone. If the member listens to you, you have regained that one. [16] But if you are not listened to, take one or two others along with you, so that every word may be confirmed by the evidence of two or three witnesses. [17] If the member refuses to listen to them, tell it to the **church**; and if the offender refuses to listen even to the church, let such a one be to you as a Gentile and a tax collector.

Did Jesus speak these words at all? Probably not. Had he spoken them to a Jewish audience, when there was no such thing as "church" in existence, he would have confused his listeners.

Obviously, the problem of settling the dispute of a "member (of the church) who refuses to listen to them" did not arise until a church was there? Since the Church did not exist yet, we can safely assume that this dialogue is set in time much earlier than when it could really have happened; and that it is a clear case of anachronism in the gospel of Matthew.

Further, the concluding words attributed to Jesus, "let such a one be to you as a Gentile and a tax collector" *don't sound like the words of Jesus at all.* They reveal a dislike or antagonism towards tax collectors with whom Jesus was accused of being too friendly; also, Jesus had learned to admire gentiles when he met the Roman Centurion, which Matthew reports ten chapters earlier.

Obviously, these words belong to someone – not Jesus – who had nursed prejudice in his heart against tax collectors and Gentiles. And, these words were, probably, put into the mouth of Jesus by someone who wanted to convince his readers of the importance of the message this passage contained.

And there are any number of such instances of interpolations, manipulations, adaptations, deletions or distortions in the Bible. It was always easy to modify, adapt, insert or delete words, phrases or even complete stories into the Bible since each copy of the Bible was produced by hand writing of copyists in those days.

Passages as these should alert the readers of scriptures of *the risks in taking its words at face value, without a deeper study or interpretation in their contexts.*

One way to be fairly sure that a particular set of words, an idea, or a message is authentically Jesus' own is when the words spoken are so very out-of-the-ordinary that it surprises or shocks the listeners of *his* time.

Like for instance, when Jesus said that it will be easier for a camel to enter into the eye of the needle than for a rich man to enter heaven. "When the disciples heard this, they were greatly astounded and said, "Then who can be saved?"" (Mat 19:25) Such reactions reveal that this statement about the rich by Jesus could not possibly be an invention of the writer.

Now, let's get back to understand the early church so we understand the Spirit of Jesus as lived out by the early followers of Jesus.

Early Church – a New Society

The disciples of Jesus, imbibed with his spirit of sharing and caring for the needy neighbors, lived as closely knit communities, taking good care of each other and their needy neighbors. They attracted a lot of people that society considered untouchables – particularly women – into their communities, as they lived a classless life. They did not discriminate between male and female, Jews and Greeks, or master and slaves.

They even sold off their properties and laid the money at the feet of their elders to hold it common. And from everyone they gathered what one could offer to the community, and to every one they gave what one needed. *They linked their profession of faith to their possession of property.*[9]

Acts 4: 34-37

[34] **There was not a needy person among them, for as many as owned lands or houses sold them and brought the proceeds of what was sold.** [35] **They laid it at the apostles' feet, and it was distributed to each as any had need.** [36] There was a Levite, a native of Cyprus, Joseph, to whom the apostles gave the name Barnabas (which means "son of encouragement"). [37] **He sold a field** that belonged to him, then brought the money, and laid it at the apostles' feet.

The Acts of the Apostles narrates in detail how they *believed material sharing to be basic to the Spirit* of Jesus they followed. A married couple, Ananias and Sapphira, after selling their property, hid part of the money and brought the rest to the community. And, they stood condemned for their deceit by Peter who told them:

Acts: 4: 4-5

---

[9] Article titled "Profession and Possession" by Robert L. (Bob)Deffenbaugh: https://bible.org/seriespage/8-profession-and-possession-acts-432%E2%80%94511

"...You have not lied just to human beings but to God."
When Ananias heard this, he fell down and died. And
great fear seized all who heard what had happened.

Not only Ananias but his wife, too, dropped dead when she came
and told the same lie. *It was death sentence by the Spirit* on those
who lied about sharing of property to the community built on
unconditional sharing and holding everything in common.

Selling off one's property is really no easy thing to do; and to
surrender the money to the group is even harder, unless the
satisfaction or the meaning the community life gave them was
proportionately greater!

What an amazing grace you witness when people so easily
"detach" themselves from their properties and follow Jesus like
sheep behind a shepherd when Jesus calls them to follow him!
For instance, Luke Chapter Five speaks of Peter, James, and Levi
"leaving everything" and following Jesus.

And, Jesus insisted that someone who wanted to follow him must
leave his luggage behind! Luke 18:22 speaks of Jesus asking the
rich young man to go sell everything and give it to the poor and
then come and follow him. And, he reports that he could not!

Surely, the early disciples were serious about sharing their wealth
in their serious attempt to live as true brothers and sisters in
Jesus, as true followers.

Loving and caring for each other, and respecting women who did
not get respect in the larger society devoid of such a spirit
attracted many new members to accept these beautiful values of
Jesus as lived out by his followers.

Indeed, the Christian message of faith, charity, and equality
before God likely appealed to the dispossessed in Roman

society. The second-century pagan writer Celsus criticized Christianity for being a religion of women, slaves, and children. Women, in particular, were given status in the early church that they did not usually enjoy in ancient society, and in many regards they were treated as equals of men. Women could serve as deaconesses, and Christianity seems to have been particularly popular among women.[10]

The community life of Jesus' followers produced a counter culture to other communities around. It gave life to societies mired in injustices, misery and brutality.

". . . Christianity served as a revitalization movement that arose in response to the misery, chaos, fear, and brutality of life in the urban Greco-Roman world. . . . Christianity revitalized life in Greco-Roman cities by providing new norms and new kinds of social relationships able to cope with many urgent problems. To cities filled with the homeless and impoverished, Christianity offered charity as well as hope. To cities filled with newcomers and strangers, Christianity offered an immediate basis for attachment. To cities filled with orphans and widows, Christianity provided a new and expanded sense of family. To cities torn by violent ethnic strife, Christianity offered a new basis for social solidarity. And to cities faced with epidemics, fire, and earthquakes, Christianity offered effective nursing services. . . . For what they brought was not simply an urban movement, but a new culture capable of making life in

---

[10] http://www.saylor.org/site/wp-content/uploads/2012/10/HIST101-6.4.2-ChristianityAndTheRomanEmpire-

Greco-Roman cities more tolerable."[11]

That's what the early Church was like, made of people who were truly the salt of the earth and the light of the world. Unfortunately we don't have such Christian communities anymore who hold all their possessions in common, share their wealth, and work towards a world without suffering and misery.

Perhaps, if there is anything left of this early Christian culture of total sharing of wealth, we may find it still being practiced among (within) the members of the Catholic Religious Communities, even today.

Members of Religious Orders give up their claim over any and all of personal earnings and property. What each one earns is pooled together and kept in common and spent according to each one's needs, and in their ministries.

In these Orders, members take a vow of 'poverty' to profess that they won't possess any personal wealth, either as property, money or in personal bank accounts.

Yet, if you suggested to these Fathers and Sisters – members of Religious Orders – to work to build a community of Christians who would gather their properties into a common pool, and share the produce according to each one's needs while contributing according to each one's capacity, they will probably identify you more as a follower of Karl Marx than as a follower of

---

[11] Rodney Stark, The Rise of Christianity, Princeton University Press, 1996, page 161 quoted at:
http://www.christianity.com/church/church-history/timeline/1-300/what-were-early-christians-like-11629560.html

Jesus.

Somewhere along the way, we have lost the message of Jesus to someone else.

And, even these members of religious Orders who truly follow Jesus' core message of leaving everything and holding their properties in common don't want their Christians to do the same, for fear of promoting communism!

Nor can these communities claim to love their neighbors as themselves, if we see the way these people who are committed to poverty living in luxury in stark contrast to the life of the poor they claim to serve.

Surely, his message to love your neighbor as yourself has been stolen away from the Christians.

The world will certainly be better if the values of Jesus were to be lived by all – that is if we believed in Jesus the way the early followers for Jesus understood and believed him.

Or, is it because we have become wiser than the apostles and the early followers that we don't leave anything to follow Jesus, and refuse to hold anything in common or to care and share with the needy neighbors?

Urgent need to reclaim the Message of Jesus for a New Society

Let us take a look at the scenario today, particularly of people whom the world considers untouchables even in this 21st century. People who are not wanted by others; those pushed to the periphery of society deprived of the most basic needs for life.

The homeless and stateless refugees number 65.3 million:
The UNHCR the UN Refugee Agency report finds 65.3 million people, or one person in 113, were displaced from their homes by conflict and persecution in 2015. "With few avenues for safe passage to seek asylum, refugees are exposed to exploitation and abuse, and their needs left without an adequate response," says the UN High Commissioner for Refugees Filippo Grandi.[12]

Those who go hungry every day are 795 million: y.
The latest available estimates indicate that about 795 million people in the world – just over one in nine – were undernourished in 2014–16.[13]

Death of kids due to lack of food every year is 3.1 million: y.
Poor nutrition causes nearly half (45%) of deaths in children under five - 3.1 million children each year.[14]

Such things happen though there is enough food to feed everyone in the world. Poverty, followed by harmful economic systems and conflicts causes these misery and death to human beings.[15]

And, today, to save the millions of our brothers and sisters from death, disease and misery, it would certainly go a long way to get

---

[12] http://www.unhcr.org/roundtable-on-protection-needs-in-the-northern-triangle-of-central-america.html

[13] http://www.fao.org/3/a-i4646e/i4646e01.pdf

[14] https://www.wfp.org/hunger/stats

[15] http://www.worldhunger.org/2015-world-hunger-and-poverty-facts-and-statistics/#produce1

that Spirit of Jesus back to our hearts and lives.

Surely, it will also help us save our own lives, because, Jesus has told us that not caring for the hungry, thirsty, homeless, and the need poor is exact same as not caring for Jesus himself; and that he will condemn us to eternal hell for such carelessness, even if we claim to be his followers.

Because they lacked in sharing everything Ananias and Sapphhira were struck down dead by his Spirit. But, today, we are left alive by the same Spirit in spite of our not caring for our hungry, naked, homeless neighbors.

May be, Jesus' Spirit is leaving us alive so we will strive to get water for the thirsty, food for the hungry, dress for the naked, shelter for the homeless, citizenship for the Stateless – and thereby secure our own lives from eternal damnation?

For, that is the ultimate promise of Jesus. For, on Judgement Day, this is how his verdict is going to be. **It won't certainly be based on one's profession of faith but by what one did with his/her possession.**

> **Mt 25: 41-45**
> 41 "Then he will say to those on his left, 'Depart from me, you who are cursed, into the eternal fire prepared for the devil and his angels. 42 For I was hungry and you gave me nothing to eat, I was thirsty and you gave me nothing to drink, 43 I was a stranger and you did not invite me in, I needed clothes and you did not clothe me, I was sick and in prison and you did not look after me.'
>
> 44 "They also will answer, 'Lord, when did we see you hungry or thirsty or a stranger or needing clothes or sick or in prison, and did not help you?' 45"He will reply, 'Truly I tell you, whatever you did not do for one of the least of these, you

did not do for me."

If that description of the Last Judgement conveys any message, one thing it makes abundantly clear is that **Jesus is not bothered about him being accurately understood as Son of God and worshipped.** But, he can't see or tolerate his poor suffer and die because those who have won't share their wealth with others. Disregarding the poor **is equal to total disregard for the PERSON of Jesus.**

In fact, Jesus who would not show off his divinity under normal circumstances; he'd even tell his disciples not to tell anyone he is Son of God.

But, even that humility of Jesus would be broken to pieces, and he would be compelled to show off his divine powers if he saw someone in need: like when he saw thousands of his followers go hungry, or when he saw a blind man, or lepers, or the body of a dead girl, a dead friend, or anyone begging for a cure, then, his divinity will show itself off, in spite of his unwillingness to flaunt his divinity.

His miracles were not a show of power; it was rather a show of his weakness to hide his divinity when confronted by the needy. Jesus wanted to teach us how to live. He was not intent on getting the largest number of followers singing his praise, larger than others in politics or religion do.

But, unfortunately, within the first three hundred years after Jesus, we find the Church leaders engaged in fierce fights to get at the right *description of Jesus.* They ended up leading the focus of their communities away from the "correct practice" (Orthopraxis) of Christianity to "correct definition/wording" (Orthodoxy).

Rather, they discovered a Jesus not as one who demands us to leave everything and follow him, nor as one who demands that we love our neighbors like ourselves, but as:

"Lord Jesus Christ, the Only Begotten Son of God, born of the Father before all ages. God from God, Light from Light, true God from true God, begotten, not made, consubstantial with the Father; through him all things were made. For us men and for our salvation…"

Certainly proclaiming loud about Jesus in so many ornamental words is a lot easier than *seeing Jesus* **in the poor people in our society and serving them by sharing our wealth.** The easier option seems to have prevailed.

But, according to Jesus, the 'content' of faith is judged by what it does to the poor and lowly. And, he even gave a demo of the 'content of faith' he expects of his followers by washing the feet of his disciples during his last meal with the community he had built of people who had left everything they had and followed him.

Surely, Jesus' choice to serve the poor and untouchables was NOT a sporadic charitable involvement in his leisure time. He was totally identified with the poor, till his last breath.

Hanging on the cross, we hear him pray a psalm from the Bible, "The prayer of a worm, not-a-man"

Mt 25: 46

And about the ninth hour Jesus cried with a loud voice, "Eli, Eli, la'ma sabach-tha'ni?" that is, "My God, my God, why hast thou forsaken me?"

This Psalm that Jesus was praying continues after another five verses:

"But I am a worm and not a man, scorned by everyone,

despised by the people."

Indeed, Jesus totally identified himself with people who were considered untouchables in his society, to his last breath — scorned by everybody, even as he was praying the prayer of such untouchables, hanging on the Cross. How much are we truly filled with the same Spirit of Jesus that anointed Jesus to serve the poor? Or, are we only calling Jesus "Lord, Lord" but forgetting to serve him in the poor he identifies himself with?

Jesus And Untouchability

6. NEW IDENTITIES OF JESUS EMERGE

The way the early followers of Jesus lived their faith as communities sharing their wealth changed in a short period of a couple of hundred years. There are specific reasons for this.

Initially, the followers of Jesus were worshipping Yahweh in the Temple and synagogues. And, they were just like any Jew of that time in their religious beliefs except that they believed the Messiah (the messenger of Yahweh) has already been sent by God, whereas other Jews were waiting for the messenger to come.

But, the early Christians were *not worshipping* the Messiah. Rather, they were busy implementing his message of sharing and caring for each other and living as a loving community. And, besides worshiping Yahweh, they would constantly remind themselves of Jesus in their breaking bread together – that is, when they ate a common meal.

To ensure their meal was in memory of Jesus, they would ask an elder who had seen and heard Jesus to share their learning experience from Jesus, even as the meal was in progress. Also, they also had made notes of such sharing by elders and read them during such meals.

The collection of these notes are what eventually evolved into the gospels we have today.

The culture of early followers of Jesus was very close to the values he taught them. And the culture of their community attracted the poor, oppressed everywhere into its fold, making the community of followers of Jesus spread fast, far and wide, and to Rome itself.

As they grew in numbers and as their peculiar style of life set them apart from the others, they were gradually perceived as an emerging threat to the existing religious and political structures, and they were feared as they could undermine Roman authority.

The God of the Followers of Jesus?

After being thrown out of the Jewish places of worship, the followers of Jesus had problem worshiping the one true God they knew, Yahweh; they could not worship their God through animal sacrifices, but they continued with their practice of breaking bread in common to remember Jesus.

Romans, who ruled over them, had a belief that their gods protected their emperor and their nation and that they should keep their gods pleased through worship and sacrifices.

They will easily adopt any god they found in the land they conquered into the pantheon of their own gods. And, they expected everyone in their nation to pay obeisance to their gods.

Romans associated worship of their gods with loyalty to the nation. But, the Jews were very adamant about worshiping only Yahweh.

For all their obduracy, Romans knew that Jews were not atheists, but meticulous worshippers of their God Yahweh.

Hence, they exempted the Jews from worshiping Roman gods.
What was meant by "impiety" or "atheism" in ancient

Greece is spelled out by Plato in his *Laws*: A citizen commits "a serious act of impiety... either by establishing a shrine in private land or by sacrificing on public land to gods not included in the pantheon of the state." We remember that in the early centuries of Christianity conversion to Christianity "could lead to a charge of 'atheism.' To opt for Christianity was also to opt for a religion that had no claim to acceptance by standards of antiquity or as a natural cult, such as Judaism had." Since Christians did not pay tribute to the god allowed or propagated to be venerated in the Roman Empire, they were outside the legitimate cultic practices and therefore face the death penalty.[16]

Christians only met in private houses for sharing bread and wine which they claimed was the flesh and blood of Jesus who was killed by the Romans on the cross. They called each other brothers and sisters. All these led to the accusation that Christians were atheists, cannibals and given to practice of incest.

Romans feared atheists as they could anger gods, and an angry god could trigger natural disasters, plagues or a defeat of their emperor in war. And, Christians are, hence, suspect and become vulnerable particularly when there was trouble in the nation.

Added to all these risks, Christians faced one more challenge. Not only deities are to be worshiped in Rome. Roman rulers too claimed to be gods.

Remember Jesus called for a coin, and asked the crowd pointedly a question about image and the inscription on the coin? "This coin had the effigy of the emperor and the superscription on one

---

[16] Hans Schwarz, The God Who IS: The Christian God in a Pluralistic World, Cascade Books, Eugene, Oregon, pp.29-30.

side: Emperor Tiberias **Son of Divine** Augustus."[17] (Emphasis added)

> Julius Caesar allowed himself to be worshiped as a god, but his successor Augustus only allowed emperor worship outside of the city of Rome. Augustus is known in some inscriptions as *CAESAR DIVI FILIUS*, Son of God, that is, Son of eternal Caesar. Oaths were taken on the divine spirit of the emperor. His image was publicly adored. Worship of the image was a regular military duty. Caligula was the first emperor to demand to be worshiped, he demanded that citizens everywhere bow to his statue.[18]

All these decades, Christians were preoccupied with the requirements of a shared life and their deep concern for the needy in society demanded of them by Jesus. But, now, they were challenged by strange demands from the world outside; to prove they were believers and worshippers of God, by worshiping Roman gods!

How else can they prove they were worshippers?

How can the followers of Jesus worship Roman gods? Jesus himself worshiped Yahweh. Early apostles and disciples worshiped Yahweh. Earlier, these Christian communities too worshiped Yahweh in the Temple, and in synagogues. Now that they can't worship Yahweh, can they start worshiping Jesus?

That would be the topic of their major debate from then on.

---

[17] David E Garland Exegetical Commentary on the New Testament – Luke; Harper Collins

[18] https://readingacts.com/2010/04/02/the-roman-cult-of-emperor-worship/

So far, Christians were content to call Jesus the messenger or messiah sent by Yahweh, or the prophet of Yahweh. They venerated Jesus for sure. But to worship Jesus as God was impossible as they truly believed in there being one and only God Yahweh.

Christians, particularly those of Jewish origin, did feel the absence of worshipping and sacrificing to Yahweh very much. And, Jewish Christians were eager to build some facility where they could offer animal sacrifices to Yahweh.

Letter to the Hebrews – No more sacrifices, please!

This Letter written, probably, by a companion of Paul and a great Biblical scholar, is a fervent appeal to the Jewish Christians **to give up their idea of building any structure to offer animal sacrifices to Yahweh**.

The appeal/argument in that letter goes like this: The worship in Jerusalem Temple is not a perfect one. Year after year, the High Priest enters its sanctuary to sprinkle animal blood to atone for *his own* and his people's sins. And, the poor efficacy Jewish of the Temple sacrifices last no longer than a year.

This Letter proposed to its readers that they see Jesus as a New High Priest. He has offered *himself* as the perfect lamb on the cross. His sacrifice, *"once and for all,"* successfully cleansed all human beings of their sins committed from the beginning of the world till the end. And, hence, **there is no need now to offer any further sacrifice to Yahweh**.

The Letter, next, addresses the question: "If Yahweh does not need to be worshiped by sacrifices, how is he to be worshiped now?" And, it answers this question thus: replace animal sacrifice with a new kind of sacrifice of praising God and doing good and sharing what you have with others.

The new Sacrifice that replaces animal sacrifice is your sharing personal wealth with others:

Heb 13: 1-3, 15,16

¹ Let mutual love continue. ² Do not neglect to show hospitality to strangers, for by doing that some have entertained angels without knowing it. ³ Remember those who are in prison, as though you were in prison with them; those who are being tortured, as though you yourselves were being tortured.

¹⁵ Through him, then, let us continually offer a sacrifice of praise to God, that is, the fruit of lips that confess his name. ¹⁶ Do not neglect to **do good and to share what you have**, for **such sacrifices** are pleasing to God.

In brief, the Letter promoted "Sharing as Sacrifice" and abolished "Animal Sacrifices."

So far so good. *The animal sacrifices associated with forgiveness of sins which Jesus rejected was rejected by this Letter.*

The Damage done by the Letter to the Hebrews

But the long arguments this Letter used to prove Jesus is a New High Priest and the title given to Jesus as a "Lamb" led to Christians associating their breaking bread in memory of Jesus into a sacrifice similar to the animal sacrifice offered in the Temple of Jerusalem.

Eventually, this letter which so well argued *against* building alters to sacrifice animals to God for our sins, ended up promoting Christians sacrificing Jesus every day to Father on the alters of Churches.

Making Jesus' death a 'sacrifice' for 'sins' negated Jesus' lifetime of a struggle to instill an awareness in the poor of being the beloved children of God the Father and live free of a nagging guilty consciousness of being in sin.

Once Christians imbibed a feeling of guilt and a self-identity of being sinners, they lost their awareness they were the beloved sons and daughters of God. A cycle of "sin>blood-sacrifice>redemption" theology took center stage, and *the blood of Jesus* became more important than any and all of his life and teachings.

Christianity became a ritual religion similar to the rituals-filled Jewish religion. The Testament Jews had with God was defined as having become Old and stale, while their own was considered New, and sealed by the blood of Jesus.

Now, Christianity has acquired a truly new identity of a full-fledged religion, exactly in the model of Judaism, laying claim to be the only true religion that replaced Judaism. And, it is only a question of time before the followers of Jesus the messiah will start worshiping Jesus as a full-fledged God.

Such transformed identity of the followers of Jesus – as if they are the newly chosen race of God who had abandoned Jews – had its strong impact on their image of Jesus, and also gave rise to Christians acquiring racist feelings against non-Christians.

Jesus who loved to call himself the "son of Man" or a "Prophet" got more sophisticated imageries and identities; Christians who spent every penny they had in caring for others, would now go hunting for souls for Christ, by subjugating and enslaving others to convert them to Christianity – which has now become the only true religion in the minds of the followers of Jesus!

Here are some phrases, titles, descriptions **used in the Letter** to describe

Jesus' identity and mission that led to the loss of the original image and spirit of Jesus.

- The Son is the radiance of God's glory and *the exact representation of his being*
- One who "had provided purification for sins"
- *"Sat down at the right hand of the Majesty in heaven"*
- *"Became as much superior to the angels"*
- Who was *made lower than the angels for a little while, but now crowned with glory and honor*
- Whom we acknowledge as *our apostle* and *high priest*.
- A *great high priest* who has *ascended into* heaven
- Jesus the *Son of God*
- *Designated by God to be high priest* in the order of Melchizedek.
- One who has *become a high priest forever*, in the *order of Melchizedek*.

That many labels were given to Jesus in one single Letter. Imagine the whole lot of literature of the books and the many letters that were in circulation in the early church (a number of them got deprecated later) and the many ways Jesus came to be 'understood' besides as lamb, Priest, Superior to Angels, Apostle, Son of God, Successor to Melchizedek, one who sits at the right hand side of the Majesty etc.

This New Identity as Priest clouds Jesus' identity as Prophet

"Types of" Sacrifice – the differentiating factor

If we'd step back again to see Jesus taking a whip to drive away everything related to animal sacrifice in the Temple, we realize that Jesus did that **not** because he thought of himself as the Lamb of God, nor because he wanted to announce that the Lamb of God has arrived, and that those inferior lambs and doves could be dispensed with?

John 2: 14-16

[14] In the temple he found people selling cattle, sheep, and doves, and the money changers seated at their tables. [15] Making a whip of cords, he drove all of them out of the temple, both the sheep and the cattle. He also poured out the coins of the money changers and overturned their tables. [16] He told those who were selling the doves, "Take these things out of here! Stop making my Father's house a marketplace!"

It was because for Jesus, God is a loving Father. He was not interested in animals. He wanted his children to come to His house to relate to Him in conversation; prayer. But, now, the priests have turned his house into a cattle market.

Jesus did not approve of sacrificing animals to a loving Father whose nature it is to forgive his children. The Father of Jesus is one who would go running out on to the street to meet the returning prodigal son or daughter, and order for a celebration to express his joy of seeing his child come back.

If Jesus' God, his loving Father, ordered for any killing of a fat goat or bull, he did it for the joy of feasting and merry making of His children! Certainly not to quench His anger by sprinkling blood!

To Jesus' Father, a prodigal child was not a sinner He disliked, hated or was very angry with; rather, the Father of the prodigal son is one who suffers daily a personal loss for missing His loving child.

What is needed of the child is a change its heart – a conversion of mind – to make a comeback. No amount of monetary gift or animal sacrifices will ever make his Father happy, but only the arrival back home of his lost child at the Father's house will satisfy Him.

When the prodigal son returned, the Father did not make him wait till the elder son – the pure one – arrived, so He can spill the pure one's blood to forgive the many sins of his younger brother. It was the good son – the Pharisee – who was upset about God not demanding penalty from His erring son.

That's how Jesus saw God his Father.

The animal sacrifices made to a blood thirsty God in the Temple made it easy for the rich to (fool themselves that they had) come clean of their sins, when they indeed continued with their oppression and exploitation of his beloved poor. And, it made it impossible for his poor to get reconciled to the loving Father at all. How sad it left the poor feeling sinful, unclean and untouchable.

And, that is what makes Jesus furious and violent. To take the whip against anyone who'd prevent God's lost children to come back home, and experience their Father's unconditional, prodigal love in silent prayerful union and embrace.

Jesus would daringly and voluntarily tell anyone who approached him with a sin-guilt-consciousness – even if the approaching person **did not** ask for any forgiveness of sins – and much to the sandal of his priests and religious leaders, "Your sins are forgiven!"

For Jesus rightly diagnosed that the poor around him lacked peace because they felt sinful and guilty, and he gave them the right medicine as a healer, all for free – the forgiveness of sins. Remember, there is no reference to his shedding blood as the Lamb of God here:

Lk 7: 37-38, 44-50

[37] And a woman in the city, who was a **sinner**, having learned that he was eating in the Pharisee's house, brought an alabaster jar of ointment. [38] She stood behind him at his feet, weeping, and began to bathe his feet with her tears and to dry them with her hair.

[44] Then turning toward the woman, he said to Simon, "Do you see this woman? I entered your house; you gave me no water for my feet, but she has bathed my feet with her tears and dried them with her hair. [45] You gave me no kiss, but from the time I came in she has not stopped kissing my feet. [46] You did not anoint my head with oil, but she has anointed my feet with ointment. [47] Therefore, I tell you, her sins, which were many, have been forgiven; hence she has shown **great love**. But the one to whom little is forgiven, loves little." [48] Then he said to her, "Your sins are forgiven." [49] But those who were at the table with him began to say among themselves, "Who is this who even forgives sins?" [50] And he said to the woman, "Your **faith** has saved you; go in peace."

Jesus claims that her many sins were forgiven because **of her great love** for Jesus expressed by kissing, anointing his feet with perfume, and **her faith – not with his blood** which will be shed soon.

Neither the Pharisee who invited Jesus to dinner, nor the woman who came to meet him saw in Jesus "the only begotten Son of God." For Jews, God did not have any son. Nowhere in the whole of the Old Testament is there a single mention of this phrase "Son of God"!

Jesus must have been understood by the people around him, like the one who invited him as a Prophet, or a Man of God, a holy person... who can help them out of the evil they suffer due to their sins: like, poverty, disease, alienation, depression...

Obviously the 'faith' that Jesus praises in this woman is her faith in God whom he re-presented in their midst; *whose presence they could experience in his presence.*

Certainly the images of Jesus as High Priest and the Lamb which got so absorbed into the popular understanding of Jesus over the years goes diametrically against the image of God that Jesus gave us, and his unique style of "distributing" forgiveness of sins for free, and very generously.

Use of Blood to Save Israelites - ordered by Yahweh?

Many centuries before Jesus, the Jews had been taken captives, and held as slaves in Egypt, and the Egyptian emperor refused to let them go free. Obviously, the God of the Jews got angry and panned to strike dead every eldest male born among humans and animals in Egypt. Sure enough, He wanted to spare his chosen children from his overnight attack.

God made a plan to ensure he won't by mistake kill children or animals of Israelites. He ordered them to kill lambs and sprinkle their blood on their door posts. Blood mark would signal God not to strike the inmates of that house, and he would pass them by. Hence this celebration of "Pass-over."
    Exodus 12: 7, 12-13

[7] They shall take some of the blood and put it on the two doorposts and the lintel of the houses in which they eat it.

[12] For I will pass through the land of Egypt that night, and I will strike down every firstborn in the land of Egypt, both human beings and animals; on all the gods of Egypt I will execute judgments: I am the Lord. [13] The blood shall be a sign for you on the houses where you live: when I see the blood, I will pass over you, and no plague shall destroy you when I strike the land of Egypt.

That whole exercise does not appear to be very rational – for God needing an identifying mark on door post to know which of the houses belonged to his chosen children. Couldn't a much simpler ID mark or proof have been invented, if God really needed one?

But, that was the original agreement/covenant between the Jews and their God – to spare them from death, sealed in blood of lambs sprinkled on their door posts!

Over the years, the blood that proved useful to be spared of punishment, and to escape the anger of God in Egypt, got linked to regular sacrifices of animals. And, eventually, it got linked to the wine shared in the **community meal** among the follower of Jesus which got defined as a new agreement/covenant with God.

Such a link to sharing of wine was gradually finding its way into **the gospels,** too; written into later on it as if Jesus himself told them that the wine was a blood sacrificed for sins.

In the narration of the Last Supper by the evangelists, instruction Jesus gave to his disciples about how they will share bread and wine are **not** uniform at all, particularly with respect to these variables:

(1) the link to wine and his blood
(2) the link to wine, his blood, and covenant
(3) the link to wine, his blood, covenant, and to forgiveness of sins

Going through the passages below, it's easy to observe how what was once a simple meal gradually got associated with blood, and later got associated with the Covenant with God, and with the blood Jesus spilled from the cross, and with forgiveness of sins.

Here are the reported wordings of Jesus about sharing wine in memorial meals:

Luke 22:17-18

[17] Then he took a cup, and after giving thanks he said, "Take this and divide it among yourselves; [18] for I tell you that from now on I will not drink of the fruit of the vine until the kingdom of God comes."

In Luke there is only mention of wine, but no link to blood, or covenant or forgiveness of sins.

Mark 14: 23

[23] Then he took a cup, and after giving thanks he gave it to them, and all of them drank from it. [24] He said to them, "This is **my blood** of the **covenant**, which is poured out for many.

In Mark there is wine, linked to blood and covenant.

Mt 26: 27-28

[27] Then he took a cup, and after giving thanks he gave it to them, saying, "Drink from it, all of you; [28] for this is my **blood** of the **covenant**, which is poured out for many **for the forgiveness of sins.**

In Matthew there is wine, linked to blood, covenant and forgiveness of sins.

John 19: 34-35

[34] Instead, one of the soldiers pierced his side with a spear,

and at once blood and water came out. [35] (He who saw this has testified so that you also may believe. His testimony is true, and he knows that he tells the truth.)

In John, there is no wine at all! **Only original blood** (of Jesus the Lamb of God) **and belief in the blood** that forgives sins.

In fact, John has no Last Supper of Jesus on the Passover Day. John's Jesus cannot eat the pascal lamb, when he himself is the Lamb of God. Hence, John advances the last evening meal Jesus had with his disciples to happen *before* the Passover

John: 13:1-3
Now before the festival of the Passover ….during supper…

When all other gospels will show Jesus celebrating Pascal Meal with his disciples as his Last Supper, John would have Jesus the High Priest offering himself as the Lamb of God on the cross, having had his last supper with his disciples, a day earlier.

The story of John about Jesus that introduced Jesus to the world through John the Baptist pointing to Jesus and saying, "Behold the Lamb of God" culminated with the Lamb of God raised on the cross as true sacrifice on the Pascal Day. For John was writing not a history of Jesus, but his theology of Jesus.

Since 'belief' is central to his theology, John strongly pleads with the reader to believe saying he is a true witness: "He who saw this has testified so that you also may believe. His testimony is true, and he knows that he tells the **truth**."

Any background to how a "belief" in blood got link to forgiveness of sins?

The concept of **the centrality of 'belief' in blood for forgiveness of sins** developed, probably, after the first three gospels were written. There were a difference of a few decades between the first three and the last gospels which was written around the years 90-110 AD.

During this intervening period "belief in Jesus" has become a matter of life and death for Christians as never before.

> Periods of peace were shattered by incidents like the great Rome fire of A.D. 64, which Emperor Nero blamed on Christians, or by the threat of external invasion, which often caused communities to close ranks.

> Christianity was punishable by death during this era, yet pardon was available to those willing to renounce their religion by offering sacrifice to the emperor or Roman gods...

> But many Christians refused to break with their faith. They were often executed and then hailed by their coreligionists as martyrs.[19]

The persecution of Christians in 64 AD meant suffering death for believing in Jesus; it meant losing beloved members of the community either to martyrdom or due to apostasy.

But, martyrdom took away life and apostasy helped one to survive on this earth. A strong theology was in need to keep the flock from bolting by turning apostates. A theology that will *boost the advantages of life after death, and depreciate life on earth of those who gave up their faith.*

Believing was certainly a matter of life and death. And, not an ordinary death: Death by being thrown to a hungry lion, being

---

19

http://www.nationalgeographic.com/lostgospel/timeline_09.html

burned alive, skinned alive, crucifixion, beheading by executioners. To motivate people to embrace such a death rather than give up, the theology needs to be really extra-ordinary, indeed.

With Jesus now understood as someone raised by God and seated at His right hand, it is becomes natural to show that those who shed blood as martyrs automatically go straight to Jesus in heaven. Getting Jesus identified as God from God, and understood as 'True' God amidst all other false gods the Romans wants them to worship makes a lot of sense in this context.

Much like the Letter to the Hebrews gave **new meaning to Jesus** as a Lamb cum High Priest, achieving martyrdom during persecution by holding on to **belief** gave **a new meaning to "discipleship of Jesus."**

Earlier, a disciple of Jesus believed in good works that will bring them closer to Jesus; the later follower believed that believing itself will take them closer to Jesus, seated in heaven above.

Early followers were challenged with sharing their property to support needy neighbors. Later followers were challenged with martyrdom/death to follow Jesus.

Today, we neither challenge ourselves to share property with needy neighbors, nor are we challenged to give up our lives for following Jesus. In this our context, we choose the easy way: Believe in Jesus and do nothing for our needy neighbors.

We prefer to believe that belief is enough, and we like to believe that we don't need to do good works or to give up our properties. Now we believe we can be "good Christians" ignoring whatever happens to the poor around, without taking any care of them.

What a distortion it is from the original Jesus and his original message, distortions due to history! What a loss that is to the suffering masses in the world.

Added factors for distortions

Interest in the life of Jesus grew in the reverse direction

When we start taking a liking to someone, we spend a lot of time talking, discussing current affairs, or situations related to the immediate life situation. As the relationship builds on, we get more interested in the history of the one we begin to love.

When Mark wrote his gospel first, he started with narration of Jesus' life from age 30. That is, from the start of his public life onwards.

As years pass by, disciples of Jesus were becoming eager to know about the childhood of Jesus, and Luke and Matthew wrote about Jesus' childhood.

And, probably, as they were written decades later, more concepts and ideas that developed about Jesus – newer theologies – influenced their writing. Matthew and Luke wrote about Jesus' infancy, and their narratives differ more than converge, indicating that a lot of theology was at play than history.

By time of Matthew, the community of followers of Jesus were getting expelled from Temples and synagogues, and Matthew was laying his claim to the rightful ownership of the Bible of the Jews, even as they were thrown out, by showing that whatever was told in the Bible was 'fulfilled' in the life of Jesus and his community.
The general thrust of Matthew's Gospel record is to

establish, on behalf of the Hebrews, that Jesus of Nazareth is the promised Messiah of Old Testament Scripture. The Greek New Testament (Aland et al. 1983) lists approximately sixty-eight Old Testament references cited in the Gospel of Matthew....

Twelve times Matthew cites Old Testament prophecy in conjunction with the term "fulfilled" ....[20]

Matthew also wanted to project Jesus as the New Moses. To show Jesus gave the new commandments to love others as oneself in a similar fashion like Moses gave the Ten Commandments on the mount Saini, Matthew changed the location of the "Sermon on the Plains" by Luke to a mountain.

Matthew presents many more similarities between Moses and Jesus: male children ordered to be killed when both were born, and only Moses and Jesus being saved; Jesus taken to Egypt to escape the death; and Moses coming to Israel to escape death; Moses sprinkling blood on people as blood of the covenant (Exodus 24:8); The blood of Jesus becoming the blood of the new covenant; both fasted 40 days; and the events surrounding birth/death of both have many similarities[21].

As years passed by, there being no written documentation of his

---

[20] Wayne Jackson, *Matthew's Use of the Term "Fulfilled"*, article *found at:* https://www.christiancourier.com/articles/1418-matthews-use-of-the-term-fulfilled

[21] For a long (complete?) list of similarities between Moses and Jesus that Matthew introduces, refer: http://www.confidentfaith.net/moses-and-jesus-devine-similarities successfully

earlier life, a lot of storytelling started doing the rounds about the childhood of Jesus, attributing extraordinary things to his younger days. There were many gospels: The Gospel of Thomas, The Gospel of James, The Gospel of Mary Magdalene, The Gospel of Bartholomew, The Gospel of Peter, The Gospel of Philip, and The Gospel of Judas.[22]

> In the second and third century we know now there were any number of gospels which had names of apostles appended to them. There were also acts or also with names of apostles appended to them so you have The Acts of Paul, The Acts of Thomas and so forth. ... these circulated quite freely in the church and Christians for a while probably used these ... somewhat indiscriminately; it's only a little bit later ... you begin to have people objecting, "don't use this one, don't use that one". ... It may surprise people to know that it's really not until the year 367 that we have a list of New Testament books that conforms exactly to the list of the twenty-seven books we would call the New Testament today.[23]

By the time John wrote his Gospel, popular interest had grown far beyond his birth to his life before his birth. And, John began his gospel saying, "In the beginning was the Word, and the Word was with God, and the Word was God. He was in the beginning with God." (John 1:1-2)

---

[22] http://wesley.nnu.edu/sermons-essays-books/noncanonical-literature/noncanonical-literature-gospels/book-of-james-or-protevangelium/

[23]
http://www.pbs.org/wgbh/pages/frontline/shows/religion/story/emergence.html

John showed Jesus was with God, and that he descended from above to ensure we *believed* in him.

With records not existing about what exactly had happened when Jesus was a child, or earlier than that, and with the large freedom writers of ancient ages enjoyed in promoting devotions by writing pious myths, the ground is rife with theological stories appearing as real history.

Between the existing Gospels, too, we could find a lot of differences that indicated how the authors edited available texts to accommodate evolving theologies.

Absorption of the image of the modified /increased Jesus as Moses (by Matthew) or God (by John), into the life and practices of Jesus' followers, over time, leads to establishing a Jewish religion in a new format. One that is devoid of the original message of Jesus who said he was anointed to bring Good News to the poor...

The followers of this New-Format-Jewish-Religion will be looking up to heaven, when Jesus was intent on bringing down heaven to earth.

Added factors for distortions

Signs leading to Belief and Blood to Forgiveness: Liberation theology of John

For John calling people to 'faith' or 'belief' in Jesus was core to his writing, and it was also the typical mindset of Christians of the post persecution era.
John 20: 30-31
[30] Now Jesus did many other signs in the presence of his disciples, which are not written in his book. [31] But these are

written so that you may come to believe that Jesus is the Messiah, the Son of God, and that through believing you may have life in his name.

John's Jesus is focused on himself, inviting others to believe in him. He goes about garnering people's faith in him, by working miracles as signs or proof of his divinity. He appears to be on a kind of an election campaign to win majority of believers and all their households into his fold.

According to John, all that it takes for one to get eternal life is believe Jesus is God. Can there be an easier way to heaven than that?

John has in fact liberated Christians from all obligations to sell off your property, share the produce with the members of your community, and to take care of needy neighbors, and shown the way to heaven by just making proclamation of your faith! Can we not call this a Theology of Liberation that freed Christians from Jesus obligations imposed on his Christians?

But, the untouchables of Jesus remain forgotten by followers of John's theology and John's gospel, too.

The only time the word 'poor' is spoken by Jesus in John's Gospel goes like this:
John 12:7-9
7 Jesus said, "Leave her alone. She bought it so that she might keep it for the day of my burial. 8 You always have the poor with you, but you do not always have me."

Jesus spoke these words to stop criticism of the woman who used costly perfume to anoint Jesus. This passage is also found in Matthew 26:11, and Mark 14:7.

What is truly significant is that John does not have any other contexts of Jesus talking of the poor copied from other Gospels into his, except this one, which Christians use to justify a life without caring for the poor – authoritatively quoting Jesus in support of their stand: the poor will always be with you!

John has no place for Jesus' statement of his mission to the poor announced by his reading from Isaiah Chapter four in the synagogue. John has very many very long sermons of Jesus, but he has no place for the teachings telling "Blessed are the Poor" or "Woe to the rich".

He has no place for the last judgement where Jesus demands of his followers not just their faith, their but active service to serve him in and through their service to the poor.

For John, those who believe in Jesus do not even come under judgement at all. Their automatically pass from death to life.
John 5: 24
Very truly, I tell you, anyone who hears my word and believes him who sent me has eternal life, and does not come under judgment, but has passed from death to life.

Faith and eternal life as understood by John related to the shedding of blood by Jesus on cross, as the sacrificial lamb. Hence, in his very first chapter, John through John the Baptist introduces Jesus as a "Lamb of God" *twice* to the readers through the words of John the Baptist: "Here is the Lamb of God who takes away the sin of the world! (v.29)" and again ""Look, here is the Lamb of God!" (v.36)

Jesus would ask for his followers to drink his blood and eat his flesh – and thus scandalize his listeners who would not drink blood of animals or humans. (John 6: 35-59)

"Lamb of God" is a very typical later Christian appellation used to mean Jesus. In the whole of the Old Testament the phrase "Lamb of God" does not occur even once. So, the audience of John the Baptist – who were not Christians – would not have understood what he meant by "Lamb of God."

In the New Testament too, this phrase "Lamb of God" occurs only twice, and only in John, and only in the two verses quoted above.

Had John the Baptist used it to introduce Jesus to the Jews who came seeking *forgiveness of their sins through his baptism* **(thereby not choosing the costly forgiveness of sins sold in the Temple by animal sacrifices)** they would not have understood what he meant. We may also ask what this Lamb of God was doing where John the Baptist was forgiving sins *without* the mandatory sacrifice of a lamb.

John the Evangelist and his Christian communities understood the life and death of Jesus as a sacrifice of the 'Lamb of God'. Hence, John the Evangelist took his liberty to construct a dialogue to introduce their beloved Jesus as a "Lamb of God" – using a hitherto unknown phrase.

Also, John's gospel reports the 'Cleansing of the Temple" incident as if it happened at the very beginning of his public life, placing it in the very second Chapter. Fast forwarding this event that occurred towards the end of the life Jesus was, probably, meant to announce that the Lamb of God has arrived, and other lambs in the Temple can now leave. We noted earlier, John also avoids showing Jesus eating the Pascal Meal as his Last Supper for the same reason and establishing the Eucharist.

John distorts an important event in the Life of Jesus

John completely disfigures the story of the Roman Centurion narrated in the Synoptic Gospels **to prove his theory that Jesus worked 'signs' (miracles) seeing which his audience 'believed' in him** – as individuals and with all of their households or communities.

1. To make sure he does not show Jesus in poor light, John avoids that part of the story about Jewish elders having to recommend the case of the Roman Centurion. For, it will prove that Jesus was not open to help non-Jews – a Jewish untouchability practice he followed religiously by excluding non-Jews from his ministry.
2. He makes the centurion **an unbelieving guy** who **personally comes to beg** Jesus to come; (Originally, he sent people to tell Jesus not to come since he was 'unworthy' – which also reveals his status as an 'untouchable' by the Jews)
3. Jesus **does not admire the faith of the non-Jew, Roman,** but rebukes/chides his unbelief saying only miracles (signs) can bring about faith in him.
4. And the **Roman officer will believe Jesus only after he confirms the healing of the sick person** in his house.

And, as usual, John concludes that he himself and all his household believed.

John 4: 47-54

[47]When he heard that Jesus had come from Judea to Galilee, he went and begged him to come down and heal his son, for he was at the point of death. [48] Then Jesus said to him, "Unless you see signs and wonders you will not believe." [49] The official said to him, "Sir, come down before my little boy dies." [50] Jesus said to him, "Go; your son will live." The man believed the word that Jesus spoke to him and started on his way. [51] As he was going down, his slaves met him and told him that his child was alive. [52] So he asked them the hour

when he began to recover, and they said to him, "Yesterday at one in the afternoon the fever left him." [53] The father realized that this was the hour when Jesus had said to him, "Your son will live." So he himself believed, along with his whole household. [54] Now this was the second sign that Jesus did after coming from Judea to Galilee.

John is more concerned with his theology than for the message of Jesus. And, he stretched the story of the Roman Centurion to suit his theology so far apart that some people wonder if the incident reported in John is the same as the one reported in Luke and Matthew.

But there are more things in common than the differences that are there. Both are about a Roman; both incidents happen in the same location. Both are placed in the larger context of belief of non-Jews. Both related to a cure of a patient not present before Jesus, etc.

This passage that was originally, painstakingly narrated in so many details by the earlier gospel writers to show how **Jesus changed his faith about non-Jews by seeing the faith this foreigner**, a Roman.

John' theological preoccupations distorted facts and leaves out these core messages from the passage:

1. Jesus's faith shaken out of its narrow view that only Jews had true faith.
2. Proclamation of Jesus that non-Jews will sit at table with Abraham, Isaac and Jacob in heaven.

Jesus had reversed his earlier belief that it is not good to throw to dogs what is meant for children (Jews), to proclaiming that all are God's children, for all have faith; in fact, people in the East or

West may be having more faith than the Jews.

What these descriptions indicate is that theologies about Jesus (Christology) grew in such a way that in less than a hundred years after Jesus, authors of the gospels had difficulty to present the open and simple personality of Jesus – a Jesus who would admire the faith of non-Jews – a Jesus who had prejudices against non-Jews but would grow out of it...

The demand of Jesus to love him in and through the poor is lost by John's preoccupation to project Jesus as God. And, his obsession with projecting multitudes of people who'd worship him after seeing his *signs*.

John projects God Jesus as busy establishing his godhood by working miracles as signs. He can't afford to see faith in others before he exhibited his godhood through miracles. The original point of this story was that the Centurion did have faith, even without seeing Jesus or his miracles – which John did miss!

May be, John could be justified given his historical situation; for those who believed in Jesus were tortured by Nero around 64 AD. You can't expect good works from Martyrs, except that they believed to the end.

Today, a person can be a great follower of Jesus by just 'believing' that Jesus is God – thanks to the theology of liberation given to us by John that liberates belief from the drudgery of action.

Jesus And Untouchability

7. FOLLOWERS OF EMPEROR'S RELIGION

Faith as "right proclamation" (Orthodoxy) than "Right Practice" (Orthopraxis)

Though the repeated and sporadic persecution Christians experienced over the first three centuries did evoke the idea of martyrs reaching heaven straight, and being in the company of Jesus, the exact status of Jesus was a matter of debate among the early Christians at least in the first three centuries.

Those who were brought up in the firm belief that there is only one God, had difficulty locating Jesus equal to God. Such people among the followers of Jesus were ready to acknowledge that Jesus was someone **similar** to God.

There were others who believed Jesus is indeed God, **same** like his Father who is God.

Those who held Jesus to be similar to God questioned the others "If Jesus the same as God the Father, then are there two Gods for Christians?"

That was a raging debate around 300 years after Jesus.

From the point of view of "Jesus and the Untouchables" that we are probing into, this debate, we must note, was **not on how best to follow Jesus who came to preach good news to the poor. But on who Jesus was? Where he was before his birth?**

Was he with the Father? In what capacity? Seated at His right hand? As a Son of God? Or, was he a man raised by God and made to sit at His right hand as the 'first born' of all creation?

What happens if someone abandons faith to escape death, due to persecution, and worshiped a Roman god — even if temporarily? Can that person be taken back to membership in the Church? Does such a person need to be baptized again, or only to be absolved of the sin? Can such a sin as apostasy ever be absolved?

Such were the intricate theological preoccupations that the churches were getting into, and often getting sharply divided on opinions.

Gradually, Jesus begins to assume personalities not known to his in his life time. For instance, we saw how Jesus became the New High Priest among Christians. It did not take long for Christians to imagine Jesus as a King, too!

In the next two centuries after Jesus, the number of the disciples swelled and the eventually, the Roman Emperor himself proclaimed that he was converting to Christianity and Christianity became the State Religion in the year 312 AD.

For the Romans, all these years, the emperor was also their god. Now, the god of the Romans – the Emperor – became a member of the Church.

With the majority of the citizens of Rome being Christians, and the unity of the nation itself was getting threatened on this fight among Christians on if Jesus was same as God or similar to God.

A divided Church is a risk to the nation's strength and its security. Hence, the Emperor takes personal interest in unifying the various sects within Christianity. In the year 325, Constantine invited all 1800 bishops with free travel and accommodation for a gathering/council at Nicaea to iron out theological differences.

"Resplendent in purple and gold, Constantine made a ceremonial entrance at the opening of the council, probably in early June, but respectfully seated the bishops ahead of himself." As Eusebius described, Constantine "himself proceeded through the midst of the assembly, like some heavenly messenger of God, clothed in raiment which glittered as it were with rays of light, reflecting the glowing radiance of a purple robe, and adorned with the brilliant splendor of gold and precious stones". The emperor was present as an overseer and presider, but did not cast any official vote. Constantine organized the Council along the lines of the Roman Senate. Hosius of Cordoba may have presided over its deliberations; he was probably one of the Papal legates. Eusebius of Nicomedia probably gave the welcoming address.[24]

At Nicaea what was attempted to be set right was the "identity" of Jesus. To put an end to all controversies **among Christians** about **who exactly Jesus is**, and eventually the Roman Christian Leaders' version prevailed over all others':

"The Only Begotten Son of God, born of the Father before all ages. God from God, Light from Light, true God from true God, begotten, not made, consubstantial with the Father; through him all things were made. For us men and for our salvation he came down from heaven..."[25]

And, any other way of understanding Jesus became heresy

---

[24] https://en.wikipedia.org/wiki/First_Council_of_Nicaea

[25] http://www.ecatholic2000.com/pray/prayer7.shtml

thereafter, and any deviation meant excommunication from the Roman Church.

Three centuries earlier, the Jews excommunicated Christians from the Temple for they refused to practice untouchability against non-Jews. That time, Christians opted to be thrown out of the Temple rather than **practice** untouchability.

Practicing Faith in Jesus then meant not minding oneself getting polluted by treating untouchables as equals – mingling with untouchables in society as equals.

Now, the Roman Christians excommunicated **fellow Christians** who would not **declare his/her faith about Jesus** exactly as was articulated by the majority bishops at Nicaea.

Practicing Faith has given way to **Professing Faith**: The Profession of faith was not in living out the values of Jesus. It was in **synchronizing the definitions of Jesus you hold in your mind with what is held in the mind by** the majority of the council fathers.

The absolute separation of belief and practice makes it very easy for one to profess one's faith without having to stand the test of practicing the values lived by Jesus and his early communities of disciples.

Today one could live under the belief that I am a great believer as I recite my creed with deep faith, and yet fail to understand the life of Jesus as one dedicated to liberation of the poor untouchables. That's how even the dedicated members of Religious Orders fail to see that building a producers' cooperative among Christians or others is more close to the values of Jesus than Karl Marx.

Have we not lost Jesus along with his message?

Jesus said that "He has sent me **to**…" Yes, Jesus came **to** us sent from God. He was someone "sent to". Sent-to-us. Emmanuel. God-with-us.

But the council of Nicaea in a sense returned Jesus back to where he came from; returned Jesus to his rightful "from" address.

After Nicaea, now Jesus is "God *from* God. Light *from* Light. True God *from* true God."

In a real sense, the humble person of Jesus who happily identified himself with tax collectors and sinners was 'rightly' defined as one who is the same as God.

This all important proper identification of Jesus took the efforts of all the bishops of the world, and the leadership of a Roman Emperor who was walking "through the midst of the assembly, **like some heavenly messenger of God**, clothed in raiment which glittered as it were with rays of light, reflecting the glowing radiance of a purple robe, and adorned with the brilliant splendor of gold and precious stones…"

The settings such as the one above with the grandeur of an Emperor, his palace, and the Bishops influence the very image of Jesus. From the original image of a friend of the worst of sinners, a new Jesus has emerged in the minds of people.

Here is one such sample of the damage caused to the original image of Jesus, beautifully brought out by a professor of theology.

A professor of Theology has a nice experience to share:
    [T]here's a beautiful mosaic in Ravenna, a city in northern

Italy, which I routinely show my classes. It's of a beautiful, very handsome, well-muscled, beardless man. He's dressed in a Roman officer's uniform. And he's stepping on the head of a lion, and he's holding a standard. And the standard says in Latin, "I am the way. The truth. And the life." And usually my students can't read Latin and I say, "Who's this a picture of?" And they guess, "The Roman Emperor." But it's not. It's a picture of Jesus. [26]

26

http://www.pbs.org/wgbh/pages/frontline/shows/religion/why/legitimization.html

8. MESSAGE OF JESUS TWISTED BEYOND RECOGNITION

Popes can err, councils can err, reformers can err. Obviously, liberation theologians can err. But we have to take the risk of praxis seeking new understanding. [27]

John Paul II claims to officially exercise his pastoral vigilance and interpret the moral teachings of Jesus in his encyclical Veritatis Splendor on 'certain fundamental questions of the Church's moral teaching', published in the year 1993. It is 182 pages long in its Indian edition. He claims this to be the first ever attempt on the topic by any pope!

[114] "... Especially today, Christian moral teachings must be one of the chief areas in which we exercise our pastoral vigilance, in carrying out our *munus regale*.

[115] This is the first time, in fact, that the Magisterium of the Church has set forth in detail the fundamental elements of this teaching, and presented the principles for the pastoral discernment necessary in practical and cultural situations which are complex and even crucial...

We critically analyze it to see:
1) Whether his pastoral discernment exercised with pastoral vigilance has anything to help solve the pastoral problem of untouchability in the Indian Church.
2) Or it turns out to be one more attempt at subverting the truth of the gospels.
The encyclical of Pope John Paul II, Veritatis Splendor, is a typical example of the way the gospel, both in parts and in Toto, is distorted to mean the opposite of whatever it stood for.

---

[27] Frederick Herzog, Justice Church, Orbis Books, Second Print, 1981, p.97

We need to go into a detailed analysis of it as it turns out to be a study, in sample, of the various types of sidetracking used throughout the centuries to camouflage the radical and liberating message of Jesus, with ill-interpreted biblical quotations.

Whatever be the result of our finding, the analysis would be valuable to discover the signs of the times. What is it that the pope is signaling? The encyclical is, in fact, replete with Bible quotations. A few hundreds of them. But the end of it all is, well-meant or ill-meant, distortion! And, this distortion will lead to such serious consequences as the continued enslavement of the untouchables.

The encyclical begins badly, argues wrongly and ends up enslaving the poor. Let us go step by step.

Wrong Beginning

The very beginning of the encyclical is off the tangent.

Its first chapter, 34 pages long, is a meditation on the Gospel narrative of the rich young man asking Jesus how to enter eternal life.

> [6]. *The dialogue of Jesus with the rich young man*, related in the nineteenth chapter of Saint Matthew's Gospel, can serve as a useful guide *for listening once more* in a lively and direct way to his moral teaching: "Then someone came to him and said, 'Teacher, what good must I do to have eternal life?' ... "

> [8].... If we therefore wish to go to the heart of the Gospel's moral teaching and grasp its profound and unchanging content, we must carefully inquire into the meaning of the question asked by the rich young man in the Gospel and, even more the meaning of Jesus's reply, allowing ourselves to be guided by them ...

That is a fantastic beginning for an epistle on Christian morality. The pope has done well in taking the encounter of the rich young ruler with Jesus to explain Christian morality.

But, when we continue to read the encyclical, we find Jesus' denunciation of the rich not even once mentioned in the entire encyclical. Jesus came out so strongly against the rich when the rich ruler went away sad. He said it would be more difficult for the rich to enter the kingdom of God than for a camel to pass through the eye of a needle. And, this denunciation came after the young man had claimed to have observed all the Ten Commandments.

Veritatis Splendor, instead, holds the rich young man as a model for all Christians.

> 7. "Then someone came to him ... "In the young man, whom Matthew's Gospel does not name, we can recognize every person who, consciously or not, approaches Christ the Redeemer of man and questions him about morality. For the young man, the question is not so much about rules to be followed, but about the full meaning of life." (Veritatis Splendor [V.S.])

Not Following Jesus —Excusable?

The episode, in Matthew's version, reads as follows:

> **Mt 19:21-27**
> 21 Jesus said to him, "If you wish to be perfect, go, sell your possessions, and give the money to the poor, and you will have treasure in heaven; then come, follow me." 22 When the young man heard this word, he went away grieving, for he had many possessions.
> 23 Then Jesus said to his disciples, "Truly I tell you, it will be hard for a rich person to enter the kingdom of heaven. 24 Again I tell you, it is easier for a camel to go through the eye of a needle than for someone who is rich to enter the

kingdom of God." ²⁵ When the disciples heard this, they were greatly astounded and said, "Then who can be saved?" ²⁶ But Jesus looked at them and said, "For mortals it is impossible, but for God all things are possible." ²⁷ The Peter said in reply, "Look, we have left everything and followed you. What then will we have?"

Veritatis Splendor describes:

²². The conclusion of Jesus' conversation with the rich young man is very poignant: 'When the young man heard this, he went away sorrowful, for he had many possessions.' (Mt 19:22). **Not only the rich man but the disciples were taken aback by Jesus' call to discipleship**, the demands of which transcend human aspirations and abilities: 'When the disciples heard this, they were greatly astounded and said, 'Then who can be saved?' (Mt 19:25). But the Master refers them to God's power: 'With men this is impossible, but with God all things are possible.' (Mt 19:26)"

It was a poignant scene to see the young man go away sad at the conclusion of his conversation with Jesus! The encyclical's empathy goes with the rich young man. It generously excuses him for not following Jesus. Further, it tries to justify the rich man by saying that Jesus demanded of him a thing that he could not do without God's power. The mistake, it is implied, is with God for not having given the power to the young man to do what Jesus demanded.

The document deliberately misleads the reader when it says: "Not only the rich man but the disciples were taken aback by Jesus' call to discipleship".

The gospels do not say that the disciples went away from Jesus or were taken aback by the condition Jesus placed before the rich man for following him. They were used to such demands which they themselves had already complied with. That was why Peter could say: **"Look, we have left everything and followed you".**

The disciples were rather shocked at his saying that it is very difficult for the rich to enter the kingdom of God. The reason for their shock was that they believed the rich could easily enter the kingdom of God, for they knew that the rich, with their money, could purchase purificatory ceremonies. 'If the rich cannot, then certainly the poor also cannot enter the kingdom', was the way their thought-pattern worked.

Jesus' reply shows that money cannot purchase salvation. On the contrary, it is the power of God that saves. It is God who saves. His power and not your money power. (Mt 19:26).

Not Naming the Rich Man

Who is this rich man? No Gospel gives his name. The encyclical observes this fact and mentions it. Mark or Luke give some details. Luke, for instance, mentions that he was a ruler (Lk 18:18).

Not giving a name is itself an indication of something that Jesus wants to say. In the parable of Lazarus and the rich man, for example, Jesus does not give a name to the rich man.

Comments *Christian Community Bible*, Catholic Pastoral Edition: (Lk. 16: 19 ff)

> A poor man named Lazarus: Jesus names the poor man, but not the rich one, thus reversing the order of the present society which treats "Mr. X" as a person but not the ordinary worker.

While the gospels thus opt not even to name him, as he was

considered unworthy of imitation by the disciples of Jesus, the encyclical projects a very positive image of the rich young man by giving him attributes nowhere mentioned in the Bible:

> [8]. The question which the rich young man puts to Jesus of Nazareth is one which rises from the depths of his heart.... The young man senses that there is a connection between moral good and the fulfilment of his own destiny. He is a devout Israelite, raised as it were in the shadow of the law of the Lord. If he asks Jesus this question, we can presume that it is not because he is ignorant of the answer contained in the law ... (VS)

The encyclical is attempting a moral thesis based on the answer to the question "What should one do to attain eternal life". Therefore, we expect the encyclical to search for all relevant passages from gospels that are related to the question.

For instance, a lawyer too asked Jesus: "Teacher what must I do to inherit eternal life?" (Luke 10: 25) This question leads Jesus to give us the parable of the Good Samaritan containing Christian morals very much directly applicable to the Indian society practicing untouchability.

But the encyclical chooses to limit itself to meditate just on the question the rich man posed to Jesus, and that, too, to Matthew's version only, completely leaving out the other two synoptic gospels.

The encyclical had to sidetrack the passage on the lawyer questioning Jesus, because its real interest was focused on the Ten Commandments and not on the new commandment of love that Jesus gave.

> [14]. This certainly does not mean that Christ wishes to put the love of neighbor higher than, or even to set it apart from, the love of God. This is evident from his conversation with the teacher of the law, who asked him a question very much like the one asked by the young man. Jesus refers him to the

two commandments of love of God and the love of neighbor (cf. Lk 10:25-
[27], and reminds him that only by observing them will he have eternal life: "Do this, and you will live" (Lk 10:28). Nonetheless it is significant that it is precisely the second of these commandments which arouses the curiosity of the teacher of the law, who asks him: "And who is my neighbor?" (Lk 10:29). The Teacher replies with the parable of the Good Samaritan, which is critical for fully understanding the commandment of love of neighbor (cf. Lk 10:30-37).
These two commandments, on which "depend all the law and the prophets" (Mt 22:40), are profoundly connected and mutually related. Their inseparable unity is attested to by Christ in his words and by his very life: his mission culminates in the Cross of our Redemption (cf. Jn 3:14-15), the sign of his indivisible love for the Father and for humanity (cf. Jn 13:1)...
. .. The Evangelist echoes the moral preaching of Christ, expressed in a wonderful and unambiguous way in the parable of the Good Samaritan (cf. Lk 10:30-37) and in his words about the final judgment (cf. Mt 25:31-46) (VS.)

The encyclical acknowledges that the lawyer's question is 'very much like the one asked by the young man'. But it does not pursue the lawyer's question because 'it is the second of these commandments which arouses the curiosity of the teacher of the law'. The encyclical tends in the direction of the first set of commandments. It is more concerned with bringing back the Ten Commandments than with discerning the love commandment.

Only once does the encyclical refer to the lawyer's question to Jesus. True, this reference does contain fine words of appreciation for the parable of the Good Samaritan. But, with that the whole episode is forgotten.

In contrast, the encyclical refers to the rich young ruler's question as many as **eleven times!** And the words 'young man' referring to the rich young ruler appear as many as **forty-one times** in the encyclical!

Jesus' Attitude towards the Rich

A key to Jesus' encounter with the young rich ruler:
To appreciate what Jesus wanted to express to the rich young ruler, we need also to see what Jesus spoke regarding the rich in different contexts.

The moral story told by Jesus of a rich man and Lazarus is one such. (Lk 16:19-31).

The rich man was just eating and drinking and wearing fine clothes. He was not going against any of the Ten Commandments! His acts are normally considered amoral. It was just *the situation of a dying Lazar* that made his eating and drinking a crime deserving hell.

According to Jesus, even if the dead Lazarus were to rise and go and warn the five rich brothers of the condemned man, they would not change; if they could not learn from the law and the prophets to share with the poor, no one could make them share their wealth.

> **Lk 16: 31**
> "He (Abraham) said to him (the rich man), 'If they do not listen to Moses and the prophets, neither will they be convinced even if someone rises from the dead.'"

Jesus' condemnation of Lazarus' rich neighbor is definitely as strong as the one about the rich in the passage the encyclical is asking us to consider in detail. *Jesus has been consistent in his teaching against the rich.*

We could see this again in the parable of the rich fool:
> **Lk 12:15-21**

[15] And he said to them, "Take care! Be on your guard against all kinds of greed; for one's life does not consist in the abundance of possessions." [16] Then he told them a parable: "The land of a rich man produced abundantly. [17] And he thought to himself, 'What should I do, for I have no place to store my crops?' [18] Then he said, 'I will do this: I will pull down my barns and build larger ones, and there I will store all my grain and my goods. [19] And I will say to my soul, 'Soul, you have ample goods laid up for many years; relax, eat, drink, be merry.' [20] But God said to him, 'You fool! This very night your life is being demanded of you. And the things you have prepared, whose will they be?' [21] So it is with those who store up treasures for themselves but are not rich toward God."

Jesus calls the rich land owner a fool because "a man's life does not consist in the abundance of his possessions." The passage about the rich young man too suggests that the young man's great possessions was the one single reason why he did not follow Jesus.

Mt 19:22
When the young man heard this word, he went away grieving, for he had many possessions.

Both these parables also deal with the question of afterlife and the preparation for it here on earth. Therefore, they too come well within the purview of the encyclical Veritatis Splendor. The answer always points to the danger of the riches.

Let us move on to pay attention to the meaning of Jesus' reply which, as the encyclical suggests, needs even greater inquiry:
[8]. If we therefore wish to go to the heart of the Gospel's moral teaching and grasp its profound and unchanging content, we must carefully inquire into the meaning of the question asked by the rich young man in the Gospel and even more, the meaning of Jesus' reply, allowing ourselves to be guided by him. (VS)

Meaning of Jesus' Replay

To study the meaning of Jesus' reply in depth, first, we need to know what exactly was said by Jesus. We have three persons reporting this particular event: Mark, Luke and Matthew.

Mark and Luke put Jesus' words into writing before Matthew did. If scripture scholars are to be believed, Matthew had used, among others, these two, Mark and Luke, as his sources.

We find some vital discrepancies between Matthew and the other two evangelists on their report of the event under consideration. Such discrepancies tend to occur often in reports related to the teachings of Jesus about the rich or the riches.

Let us compare, for example, the reporting by Luke and Matthew on the sermon on the 'mount':
Lk 6:20
... "Blessed are you who are poor, for yours is the kingdom of God."

Lk 6:24
"But owe to you who are rich, for you have received your consolation."

Matthew, when narrating the above teaching of Jesus (Sermon on the Mount) would expand the word "poor" as "poor in spirit" and omit the "owe to you who are rich":
Mt 5:3
"Blessed are the poor in spirit, for theirs is the kingdom of heaven"

The presence of rich people in the congregation addressed by Matthew is surmised to be the reason for the above said expansion as well as omission.

In the case we are studying now, Mark reports the reply of Jesus to the rich young man, after the rich man claims to have observed the commandments, as:

Mk 10:21

Jesus, looking at him, loved him and said, "You lack one thing; go, sell what you own, and give the money to the poor, and you will have treasure in heaven; then come, follow me."

And Luke as:

Lk 18:22

When Jesus heard this, he said to him, "There is still one thing lacking. Sell all that you own and distribute the money to the poor, and you will have treasure in heaven; then come, follow me."

Jesus is seen here refusing to accept observance of the Ten Commandments as the sufficient condition for reaching eternal life. There is something lacking still.

Matthew's report:

Mt 19: 21

Jesus said to him, "If you wish to be perfect, go, sell your possessions, and give the money to the poor, and you will have treasure in heaven; then come, follow me."

Matthew has removed the words, 'you lack one thing' of Mark and 'one thing you still lack' of Luke from Jesus' lips. Yet, even Matthew could not completely omit the words of Jesus in his narration. He places these words in the mouth of the rich young man:

Mt 19:20

The young man said to him, "I have kept all these; what do I still lack?"

Matthew's concern for the rich Christians in his Church seems to have made him put the words of Jesus into the mouth of the rich young ruler. For that reason, he also makes the command of Jesus to sell and give to the poor, look like an if-you-wish-you-may-do kind of an 'option'.

Still, Matthew does not omit the condemnation of the rich by Jesus. Nor does he explain why Jesus should say such a harsh statement against the rich. After all, the rich man had observed the commandments and he had only not made an option which according to Matthew's rendering is, anyway, just optional.

What exactly is the Demand of Jesus?

The point gets clarified further when we analyze what Luke, Mark and Matthew include in the commandments in the reply of Jesus.

Mk 10:17-20

[17] As he was setting out on a journey, a man ran up and knelt before him, and asked him, "Good Teacher, what must I do to inherit eternal life?" [18] Jesus said to him, "Why do you call me good? No one is good but God alone. [19] You know the commandments: 'You shall not murder; you shall not commit adultery; you shall not steal; you shall not bear false witness; you shall not defraud; Honor your father and mother.'" [20] He said to him, "Teacher, I have kept all these since my youth."

Lk 18:18-21

[18] A certain ruler asked him, "Good Teacher, what must I do to inherit eternal life?" [19] Jesus said to him, "Why do you call me good? No one is good but God alone. [20] You know the commandments: 'You shall not commit adultery; you shall not murder; you shall not steal; you shall not bear false witness; Honor your father and mother. ", [21] He replied, "I have kept all these since my youth."

Mt 19:16-21

[16] Then someone came to him and said, "Teacher, what good deed must I do to have eternal life?" [17] And he said to him, "Why do you ask me about what is good? There is only one who is good. If you wish to enter into life, keep the

commandments." [18] He said to him, "Which ones'?" and Jesus said, "You shall not murder; you shall not commit adultery; you shall not steal; you shall not bear false witness; [19] Honor your father and mother; also, you shall love your neighbor as yourself." [20] The young man said to him, "I have kept all these; what do I still lack?" [21] Jesus said to him, "If you wish to be perfect, go, sell your possessions, and give the money to the poor, and you will have treasure in heaven; then come, follow me."

According to Mark and Luke, Jesus **directed** the young man to only the observance of the Ten Commandments, whereas in Matthew: **to keep** the Ten Commandments **together with** the new commandment to love one's neighbor.

According to Matthew, thus, the young man's claim to have observed all the law means a claim to have observed all **Ten Commandments plus the new commandment of love.** According to Mark and Luke, he had claimed to have observed **the Ten Commandments** only. That makes a world of a difference.

If one can stand before Jesus and dare say that he/she has loved his neighbor as himself/herself then that person hardly lacks anything. Nothing more can be obligatory. That seems to be the position of Matthew. But, the position of Mark and Luke seems to be as follows: if one limited oneself to observe only the negative commandments, then one should beware! These commandments are not enough. Any complacency rising out of observing just the Ten Commandments, without the commandment of love, could land the person in hell. According to Luke and Mark, Jesus is saying the Decalogue is necessary but not sufficient.

This interpretation is in line with what a Father of the Church, Basil, observes.

The Demand of Jesus as Basil the Great Sees

St. Basil, (c.330-379), comments on this encounter of the rich young man with Jesus, as follows:

(It) ... deals with the Christians who, like the young man in the gospel, keep all the other commandments but forget the most important one:

Though you have not killed, . . . nor committed adultery, nor stolen, nor borne false witness, you make all of this useless unless you add the only thing which can allow you to enter the kingdom ... If it is true that you have kept the law of charity from your childhood, as you claim, and that you have done so much for others as for yourself, then where does all your wealth come from? Care for the poor absorbs all available resources ... **So whoever loves his neighbor as himself owns no more than his neighbor does.** But you have a great fortune. How can this be, unless you have put your own interests before those of others ... I know many people who fast, pray, groan, and do any kind of pious work that doesn't affect their pockets, but at the same time they give nothing to the needy. What good are their merits? The kingdom of heaven is closed to them... [28]

Thus, according to Basil, the observance of all the Ten Commandments along with any amount of prayer and fasting does not open the doors of heaven if one lacks in the practice of love of neighbor as oneself which results in not being rich.

We can compare this with the conclusion arrived at by Veritatis Splendor to understand the latter's sidetracking:

[13] ... From the context of the conversation, and especially

---

[28] St. Basil, Homilia VII, 1,3 and 4, MFG, T.XXXI, Cols. 280-281, 288,289-292 as quoted by John C.Cort, Christian Socialism, Orbis, 1988, 2nd edition.

from a comparison of Matthew's text with the parallel passages in Mark and Luke, it is clear that Jesus does not intend to list each and every one of the commandments required in order to "enter into life", but rather wishes to draw the young man's attention to the "centrality" of the Decalogue with regard to every other precept, inasmuch as it is the interpretation of what the words "I am the Lord your God" mean for man. (VS.)

While, according to St. Basil, the encounter with the rich man proves the insufficiency of the Ten Commandments for reaching one to God's kingdom, according to Veritatis Splendor, the same event proves the centrality of the Decalogue.

Veritatis Splendor chooses Matthew because it is in Matthew alone that Jesus says "Keep the commandments", while in Mark and Luke, Jesus just says 'You know the commandments".

Matthew's intention seems to be to project Jesus as the New Moses. Hence, Matthew's Jesus demands that one should observe the commandments: the ten plus the commandment to love.

After full 82 pages of analysis, all that Veritatis Splendor could say is:

> [52] ... The Church has always taught that one may never choose kinds of behavior prohibited by the moral commandments expressed in negative form in the Old and New Testaments. As we have seen, Jesus himself reaffirms that these prohibitions allow no exceptions: "If you wish to enter into life, keep the commandments . . . You shall not murder, you shall not commit adultery, you shall not steal, you shall not bear false witness" (Mt 19: 17-18).

Strangely the encyclical omits the words in the next verse of Matthew (19: 19) "Honor your father and mother, and, you shall love your neighbor as yourself."

The pope seems to take great pleasure in knowing that Jesus, as a New Moses, has given us the Ten Commandments back.

> [12] ... From the very lips of Jesus, the new Moses, man is once again given the commandments of the Decalogue. Jesus himself definitively confirms them and proposes them to us as the way and condition of salvation.

The new Moses, according to Matthew, demands the observance of **eleven** commandments. But the encyclical has censored the new Moses of the eleventh commandment and thereby retains Jesus as the old Moses himself.

> [52].... The negative precepts of the natural law are universally valid. They oblige each and every individual, always and in every circumstance. It is a matter of prohibitions which forbid a given action *semper et pro semper*, without exception ... (VS.)

Ten Commandments Central for Salvation?

The laws given by Moses are many. Even when the prohibitory ones are taken separately, there are more than just ten prohibitory commandments given by Moses. The Pharisees confronted Jesus with these prohibitory laws when they found Jesus breaking them.

Jesus did not observe all the negative, prohibitory commandments of Moses either. He chose what to observe and what not to. For instance, he broke the laws that prohibited touching a leper, working on a Sabbath, or touching a woman in her menses. He broke them positively, and in public, to the scandal of his religious leaders.

Jesus had also explicitly said that the demands of the prohibitory negative commands of Moses are not at all sufficient. For example:

Mt 5:21-22

[21]"You have heard that it was said to those of ancient times, 'You shall not murder': and 'whoever murders shall be liable to judgement.' [22] But I say to you that if you are angry with a brother or sister, you will be liable to judgement; and if you insult a brother or sister, you will be liable to the council; and if you say, 'You fool,' you will be liable to the hell of fire."

Mt 5:27-28

[27]"You have heard that it was said, 'You shall not commit adultery.'[28] But I say to you that everyone who looks at a woman with lust has already committed adultery with her in his heart."

We saw how Paul, following Jesus' trend, would break commandments that prohibited eating certain food, or associating with uncircumcised people. Jesus could sift through the volumes of Mosaic Law with the help of the commandment to love one's neighbor. Even this love of neighbor, if we follow Jesus' way of approaching situations, has to be seen in the light of people's history, in the light of the signs of the times.

But, Veritatis Splendor is categorical in saying that Jesus allowed no exceptions to the laws he gave to the rich man in Matthew's Gospel. How does one account for the omission in the Veritatis Splendor of the new commandment given by Jesus in the same Matthean narration? Did Jesus give the commandment of love of neighbor as just an option that one might or might not choose to follow?

The Love Command Optional? If you wish to be perfect. . .

Unlike what Veritatis Splendor claims, to be perfect is not an option given to the rich young man.

Mt 5: 48

"Be perfect, therefore, as your heavenly Father is perfect."

Jesus commands us to be perfect. The rationale for this is: "so that you may be children of your Father in heaven ... (Mt 5: 45)". Yet, one may opt not to be a child of God! One may choose to be a bastard!

One cannot choose to be a child of God and still not sell and share one's property with the poor!

Being perfect, being a child of God and being a disciple of Jesus - all imply that one should sell one's property and distribute the money to the poor. Selling and distributing to the poor is the only authentic way of living the love commandment.

Because of its obsession with the negative commandments, the encyclical misses the message of Jesus. It seems to openly acknowledge that the Church has never taken seriously the positive commandment. All it boasts of is that the Church has always taught never to choose against the Ten Commandments.

The Church Has Always Taught. . .

After all, there is nothing to be so proud of in saying that the Church has always taught the negative commandments. The Church could not have taught otherwise anyway - like, for instance: "Go and Kill" or "Commit adultery".

The negative commandments, if breached, disqualify one not only from eternal life, so the encyclical seems to think, but also from earthly life itself! One will have to face electric chair or the hang-man's noose for breaching such commandments. The encyclical seems, at best, to be teaching people the way to escape capital punishment and survive in this earth and not showing the way to the kingdom of God.

A Bad Student of a Good Teacher?

A good teacher acts as a "midwife". She does not deliver the truth. But helps the truth in the other to unfold itself.

When a rich young ruler approaches him, Jesus as a good teacher is obviously trying to elicit from the questioner what he thinks he already knows. The teacher leads the seeker from what he knows to what he does not know: from the false security of the Ten Commandments to the challenges of the commandment to love one's neighbor as oneself.

Veritatis Splendor has obviously missed the point so sorely that it leaves out the conclusion of the episode reported by all the three synoptic gospels. The conclusion says that the rich cannot enter heaven without shedding their load of wealth; that it is harder for the rich to enter heaven than for a camel to go through the eye of a needle. Not even once does the camel get mentioned in the 182 pages of the meditation cum analysis of this encounter of the rich young man with Jesus. The encyclical is a classic case of staining a gnat and missing the camel!

Why the Ten Commandments?

The Ten Commandments cannot be set even as any lower limit to reach heaven. The revolutionary teaching of Jesus is that even those commandments were only an expression of the commandment to love, applied to a group of people at a point of time.

Even Yahweh does not seem to have taken the commandments He gave all that seriously. Take the case of Moses. If Yahweh chose him to lead the Israelites, was it not because Moses loved his clan to the extent of murdering an Egyptian? God who heard the cry of the people responded by choosing just this murderer to liberate them.

If rather Veritatis Splendor is to be taken seriously, the Bible should read like:

Yahweh appeared to Moses and said, "Don't come near me, you a murderer! I, Yahweh, prepared you all these years to present the Ten Commandments to the people of Israel. Now how can I do that? Will not people laugh at me and say, 'The very guy who had committed a murder is chosen to give us the commandment not to murder?' Get lost from me, you who have destroyed my wonderful plan of salvation history!

And therefore Yahweh destroyed Moses and waited for John the Baptist to come before he would give the Israelites the Ten Commandments.

Again, the very people Yahweh was interested in redeeming were committing the mortal sin of murdering their male children at the very time that he wanted to save them! Yahweh was **in fact more concerned about saving his children from the very situation of having to murder their male children.** He was not in the least appearing to be offended that they were committing the mortal sin of murdering their children. He was rather sorry for their plight, for their situation. His effort was to change their situation to one in which they could see their children grow.

The encyclical could not think of any such situation where one might not be condemned by Yahweh for having broken His laws. The encyclical's Yahweh is so cruel that if you want to be in His company, you should prefer to rather die than go against His commandments:

> [94] ... The words of the Latin poet Juvenal apply to all: "Consider it is the greatest of crimes to prefer survival to honor and out of love of physical life, to lose the very reason for living." (VS.)

It is very significant that Veritatis Splendor had to go outside the entire Bible to find a quotation from Juvenal to justify its stand.

> [52].... The negative precepts of the natural law are universally valid. They oblige each and every individual, always and in every circumstance. It is a matter of prohibitions that forbid

a given action *semper et pro semper*, without exception, '"
(VS.)

But Yahweh's concern was more for the people than for His
commandments. He understood His commandments as
instructions given in the interest of His people:

Jer 7:23

But this command I gave them, "Obey my voice, and I will be
your God, and you shall be my people; and walk only in the
way that I command you, **so that it may be well with you."**

Jesus reflects the same concern of Yahweh when he was fighting
the theology of the Pharisees. Jesus was trying to create a new
world, God's kingdom, where people will not have to commit
sins. Jesus was interested in the sinners; and not so much in
saving the moral theology of the Pharisees even though it was
considered to be founded on the Bible.

Paul continued this same mission of Jesus when he fought the
theology of the party of the Christian Pharisees from Jerusalem.

Jesus' approach was to discern the pastoral situation he was in,
and to understand what the Commandment of God implied in
that situation. He could think of situations, wherein little ones
could be caused to sin, very much like the Israelites having had
to kill their first born. The thing to do, according to him, in such a
situation is:

Mt 18:6

"If any of you put a stumbling block before one of these little
ones who believe in me, it would be better for you if a great
millstone were fastened around your neck and you were
drowned in the depth of the sea."

Doesn't Jesus appear here to advocate the kind of behavior
prohibited by the negative moral commandments?

Again, faced with the question of the negative, prohibitory Law

of Moses that forbade work on a Sabbath Jesus would ask:
Lk 14:5-6
⁵ ... "If one of you has a child or an ox that has fallen into a well, will you not immediately pull it out on a Sabbath day?" ⁶ And they could not reply to this.

Jesus' question stretches situational ethics to the farthest extreme. He is not just explaining a situation in which a poor man may not be guilty even when breaking a law; he is almost saying that the instance of the teacher's breaking a law makes it legitimate for people to break the law! 'If you can break laws, why not we?' - appears to be the question of Jesus. In other words: if you can have situational ethics, i.e., meaningful exceptions to the rule, why not think of possible exceptions to the underprivileged also?

Jesus would even go much further:
Mt 21:31-32
³¹ ... Jesus said to them, "Truly I say to you, the tax collectors and the prostitutes are going into the kingdom of God ahead of you (the chief priests and elders). ³² For John came to you in the way of righteousness and you did not believe him, but the tax collectors and the prostitutes believed him; and even after you saw it, you did not change your minds and believe him."

Jesus is not contrasting one priest against one prostitute. He is talking of the chief priests and the prostitutes as one class opposed to the other. Surely, the prostitutes' going ahead of the chief priests to heaven can never be explained if one bases oneself on the Ten Commandments.

The high priests believed the prostitutes were sinners. Jesus rather believed that the high priests and elders were responsible for the situation that caused those women to sin. Evidently, in Jesus' opinion, not exercising one's responsibility to do good could be worse than doing evil!

Even holy people, occupying responsible positions could be causing little ones to sin with their obsession with preaching the Ten Commandments, instead of doing something to remove the situation that causes them to sin. They should be held responsible for the sins committed by the poor.

Where does the Encyclical Go Wrong?

Veritatis Splendor say.

> 17. We do not now know how clearly the young man in the Gospel understood the profound and challenging import of Jesus' first reply: 'If you wish to enter into life, keep the commandments'. But it is certain that the young man's commitment to respect all the moral demands of the commandments represents the absolutely essential ground in which the desire for perfection can take root and mature, the desire, that is for the meaning of the commandments to be completely fulfilled in following Christ.

If, as the encyclical says, Jesus asked the young man to observe only the Ten Commandments, definitely then, there is nothing very profound about the first reply of Jesus. The Ten Commandments are expected to be followed by any decent human being in a civilized society. All the gospels agree that the young man replied Jesus saying that he observed all the commandments.

Mark gives us the reaction of Jesus when the rich man responded to his reference to the Ten Commandments:

Mk 10:20-21

20 He said to him, "Teacher, I have kept all these since my youth." 21 **Jesus, looking at him, loved him** and said "You lack one thing ...",

163

There is no need for the encyclical to doubt 'how clearly the young man in the Gospel understood the profound and challenging import of Jesus' first reply'. The real problem is with the second reply of Jesus.

Here, too, all the synoptic gospels report unanimously that the rich man understood Jesus perfectly well. That was why he left Jesus and went away sorrowful! If the rich young man had understood Jesus as did the encyclical, he need not have gone away sorrowful at all! He could simply have told Jesus: "Thank you for the invitation. Sorry, I am not interested in being perfect." And Jesus should have appreciated his decision since God has not given him the grace to be perfect! Jesus, in that case, need not have made such horrible remarks on the rich after he left him!

Encyclical under Compulsion?

The concern seems to be more for bringing back the Mosaic Law and the council of Trent than for focusing on the new law given by Jesus. And that makes the encyclical, as we have seen earlier, compelled to stick to

Matthew's version only (minus verse 19)! But even here the concern is to be faithful more to the council of Trent in its hairsplitting exercise of differentiating between mortal and venial sins than to the narration of Matthew itself.

Says Veritatis Splendor:
> [68]. .,. As the Council of Trent teaches, "the grace of justification once received is lost not only by apostasy, by which faith itself is lost, but also by any other mortal sin."
> *Mortal sin and venial sin*
> [69]. As we have just seen, reflection on the fundamental option has also led some theologians to undertake a basic revision of the traditional distinction between mortal sins

and venial sins...(V.S)

Trent and the Church traditions safeguard the rich. The theology contained in Trent was conducive for Christians to capture as animals the whole population of Africa and sell them among Christians to work in their farms. With such a theology, the Church leaders could afford to keep silence even as Jews faced genocide at the hands of 'Christians'! With all its concern for the Ten Commandments and the theology taught by Trent, the Church could bless murder and looting by Christian kings while colonizing country after country in Asia, Africa and the like.
To quote Bhulmann:

> Certainly we know that many Bulls sent by popes in the 15th and 16th centuries to the Portuguese and Spanish monarchs sought to give gentler, more humane character to colonial ventures nonetheless. Alexander VI, in Inter Cetera, 1493, 'with the authority almighty God has granted us' did entrust the new worlds to the two kings and their successors, 'for all time' so that they might 'subjugate the barbarian' peoples and bring them to the faith. From then until the last colonial undertaking, the conquest of Abyssinia in 1935-36, the Church never raised a formal protest against colonization.[29]

Naturally, the Christian monarchs would not be able to conquer the infidels and subjugate them without killing those who resisted. The then Pope evidently presumed that killings by monarchs did not contravene the dictates of the negative prohibitive commandments of the Decalogue.

Right now our suffering is under the modern version of colonialism. The new colonizer is not any king who wants permission from the pope to commit murder and looting. The

---

[29] Frederick Herzog, Justice Church, Orbis Books, Second Print, 1981, p.97

new colonizer, rather, has perfected his tools of exploitation. He does not have to plunder and loot to acquire more wealth. See what the Catholic Pastoral Edition of the Christian Community Bible comments under the story of the rich man and Lazarus in Luke 16: 19ff.

In several countries, the privileged minorities have not only taken over the table to which everyone was entitled: power, the laws and the culture, but they have also organized the country's economy in a way that suits them. They have even destroyed the national industries and job opportunities. Their country's economic dependence enables them to continuously feast, while condemning millions of Lazarus to unemployment, and consequently, to being progressively marginalized until they die of hunger and destitution.

The new colonizer has trapped poorer nations into deep debts by engineering arms race around the world, and by breaking open doors to dump his consumer goods.

He need not take things away by plunder any more. The poor nations will have to export to survive - export food to the rich nations even at the cost of their poor dying of hunger, export clothes even when their poor go naked.

This new colonizer too needs popes to help him out as he fears the rebellion of the poor. The poor have to be made to feel so low that they don't revolt. They have to be made rather to accept their poverty as the effect of their sins than to realize that they are forced to lead sinful lives because of their economic slavery. To make them feel sinful and guilty, insistence on the Ten Commandments comes handy. Feeling guilty and sinful, the poor could be expected to watch passively their Government export food, clothing, raw materials etc.

Can Law be called into Question?

When a street child says that it lives only by stealing, or when a young woman says she lives as a sex worker, one is led to question the very relevance of the Ten Commandments to their situation.

The Catholic Pastoral Edition of the Christian Community Bible comments under the story of the rich man and Lazarus in Luke 16:19ff.

> Modern-day Lazarus is kept at a distance from the residential areas by police, dogs and barbed wires. He would like to get his fill of the crumbs which are left over from the feast, but there are few crumbs 'falling' back to the homeland, after everything is wasted on imported products or deposited in foreign banks. Lazarus lives among rubble and rubbish: he becomes a prostitute, or a pickpocket, until a premature death enables him to find someone who loves him: at the side of Abraham and the angels. And at last, he will find a home where others will not be able to strip him, watch him, and beat him in the name of their own security.

But, questioning law does appear criminal. Those who questioned could be termed unfaithful to the Bible. And people who make much of situational ethics could appear to be led by the flesh!

But it would help to keep in mind that the first Jerusalem council did dare to reject laws sacred to the Jews.

Acts 15:10

Now therefore why are you putting God to the test by placing on the neck of the disables a yoke that neither ancestors nor we have been able to bear?

Peter is thus speaking about the Mosaic Law! Veritatis Splendor would rather tell Peter:

[18] "Those who live 'by the flesh' experience God's law as a burden, and indeed as a denial or at least a restriction of their own freedom. On the other hand, those who are

impelled by love and 'walk by the Spirit' (Gal 5: 16), and who desire to serve others, find in God's law the fundamental and necessary way in which to practice love as something freely chosen and lived out." (VS.)

Veritatis Splendor here quotes just four words of Paul from Galatians 5: 16 to support adherence to the Mosaic Law: 'walk by the Spirit'. But out of context. What Paul wanted to convey was just the opposite.

Gal 5: 16-18

[16] Live by the Spirit, I say, and do not gratify the desires of the flesh. [17] For what the flesh desires is opposed to the Spirit, and what the Spirit desires is opposed to the flesh; for these are opposed to each other, to prevent you from doing what you want. [18] But if you are led by the Spirit, you are not subject to the law.

The question is not whether to observe the law or not. Obviously one should not murder, rape or cheat. The question is about taking refuge in observing just the Ten Commandments. This is what is being challenged by Jesus, by Peter and by Paul.

The call of Jesus, Peter and Paul is to walk by the spirit. Not to feel secure by examining one's conscience on the Decalogue of Moses. Those who walk by the spirit cannot be satisfied with the law. Nor are they under it. They discern and even go beyond the law.

When Jesus says, "Do not think that I have come to abolish the law and the prophets; I have come not to abolish but to fulfill." (Mt. 5: 17) Jesus is not in any way claiming that if he had wanted to he could have abolished the law! What he rather says is that the law is not sufficient for the kingdom. Laws lack a lot and he is going to fill up whatever was lacking.

The question that should have been asked is "What is the Christian way of fulfilling what is lacking in the law?" That is the only relevant question for Christian morality and it is precisely here that Veritatis Splendor fails miserably.

The Problem in its Context

After all, what they have failed is in doing certain good actions. Not doing good actions is not as bad as doing forbidden actions according to the encyclical:

> [52] ... On the other hand, the fact that only the negative commandments oblige always and under all circumstances does not mean that in the moral life prohibitions are more important than the obligation to do good indicated by the positive commandments. The reason is this: the commandment of love of God and neighbor does not have in its dynamic any higher limit, but it does have a lower limit, beneath which the commandment is broken. Furthermore, what must be done in any given situation depends on the circumstances, not all of which can be foreseen; on the other hand there are kinds of behavior which can never, in any situation, be a proper response - a response which is in conformity with the dignity of the person. Finally, **it is always possible that man, as the result of coercion or other circumstances, can be hindered from doing certain good actions; but he can never be hindered from not doing certain actions, especially if he is prepared to die rather than to do evil**." (V S.)

We would say command to love, when obeyed, makes one good. A Samaritan who loved his wounded neighbor became the Good Samaritan. But this command, according to the tenor of Veritatis Splendor, is optional. Such a position leads to anomalous responses. Say, if priests and nuns sacrifice their lives and become celibates to serve others they are doing good. But if 'as a result of coercion or other circumstances', like caste prejudice which is a cultural coercion, they are 'hindered from doing certain good actions', such as admitting Dalit Christians in their institutions, it is always 'possible' for Veritatis Splendor to condone them.

Acts without Actors

Acts that contravene the spirit of the commandments could well be called sinful. Such acts could be condemned. But such a condemnation presumes that the actors freely chose to act the way they did. The Spirit of Jesus would keep calling Christians to have compassion.

Veritatis Splendor's refusal to look into the circumstances under which evil is 'chosen' ends in its condemning the victims of evil and condoning the perpetrators of evil.

Here again, Veritatis Splendor quotes Vatican Council II Documents to prove the opposite of what was intended:

[80] ... without in the least denying the influence on morality exercised by circumstances and especially by intentions, the Church teaches that 'there exists acts which *per se* and in themselves, independently of circumstances, are always seriously wrong by reason of their object'. The Second Vatican Council itself, in discussing the respect due to the human person, gives a number of examples of such acts: (VS.)

[80] ... "Whatever is hostile to life itself, such as any kind of homicide, genocide, abortion, euthanasia and voluntary suicide; whatever violates the dignity of the human person, such as mutilation, physical and mental torture and attempts to coerce the spirit; whatever is offensive to human dignity, such as subhuman living conditions, arbitrary imprisonment, deportation, slavery, prostitution and trafficking in women and children; degrading conditions of work which treat laborers as mere instruments of profit, and not as free responsible persons: all these and the like are a disgrace, and so long as they infect human civilization they contaminate those who inflict them more than those

who suffer injustice, and they are a negation of the honor due to the Creator" (VS.)

[81] ... Consequently, circumstances or intentions can never transform an act intrinsically evil by virtue of its object into an act "subjectively" good or defensible as a choice. (VS.)

Let us underscore the words of Vatican II: *They contaminate those who inflict them more than those who suffer injustice.*

While the Vatican II Document is focusing its attention on the situation and locating the guilt of those who inflict evil, Veritatis Splendor keeps condemning the victims by focusing on the act itself.

That leads us to ask how an act could become intrinsically evil without having any reference to the context. Let us take adultery for an example. As such, it is an act of sex acted outside the context of marriage. The same act, when done within marriage becomes the consummation of the sacrament of marriage.

If the situation does make a difference, as in the example we are considering here, then there could be degrees of intensity of guilt. A rich man's having sex in a brothel does not equate with that of a woman or a child who is playing his partner. One is there for pleasure and the other is there in spite of the pains and misery and the nausea. We are not trying to glorify adultery or prostitution here. But we are saying that if prostitution or adultery is dehumanizing the persons who are at it, then the responsible way of approaching the problem would be to ask: why this happens? And what is to be done to help people make humanizing choices?

Such people as are not free to choose a life in keeping with their human dignity are the focal concern of Jesus for his preaching the good news of the kingdom. What is important is that a person must have an opportunity to live a life worthy of a human being.

To create a world of that kind, "the kingdom of God", is the moral obligation of all the people of the world. An obligation never spoken of in the encyclical. Until one has tried to create that world, one has no moral rights to preach morality. Let no one add insult to injury by condemning the victims pushed into sin, asking them to commit suicide by quoting Juvenal!

Discernment is a must since ethics is always situational. The pastoral discernment of the pope exercised with pastoral vigilance has taken him back to Moses' Decalogue and to the council of Trent. Perhaps the pastor-author of Veritatis Splendor had no real community of Christians with whom he could exercise discernment. This pastor is so far removed from the lives and struggles of Dalit Christians that it is no point in expecting a pastoral discernment from him either.

Probably, if this pastor could sit with his bodyguards who keep away the little ones from coming near him and discern the relevance of the Decalogue with them, he might discover that he is kept alive by the readiness of his bodyguards to violate one of the Ten Commandments: "Do not kill". The bodyguards are under instructions to violate this command on spotting a potential assassin. If the pope can allow his bodyguards to ignore the ten commandments of Moses to protect his own physical life, why not the poor Christians have some situational ethics to protect their interests?

9. CHRISTIANITY BEYOND AND THROUGH NICENE CREED

Over the centuries, particularly after the council of Nicaea the image of Jesus the Prophet got projected as a meek lamb whose only purpose to have visited the earth was to shed blood, in place of the lambs Israelites were offering and to gather 'believers' in the mystery of God's anger cooling off after seeing Jesus' blood.

All that one needed to do is to 'believe' Jesus is God. Nothing else is important. How you live, what you do with your wealth are not anyone else's concern than your own. Concern for your neighbor is no more important to be a good Christian. Jesus can be followed today by following Church rituals that have perfectly replaced the Temple rituals.

The King Jesus and his diverted Mission

When asked what one should do to attain eternal life, Jesus told us the story of the Good Samaritan. And gave the commandment: Go and do like that Samaritan if you want to be redeemed.

The very early Christian communities were made of such people who loved each other. People knew them as Christians because of their love and support for one another in every way. And as we saw just a few pages back, they were people who created a new culture of care. Just like the Good Samaritan.

But, now with Jesus defined as a powerful king, Christians who originally refused to join the military and refused military service membership in Christian communities now have to defend their King and kingdom. They could become agents of the empire in its mission to defend itself or partake in the expeditions of emperors to expand their territory – the territory of Jesus' kingdom: The Roman Empire!

Thus we got a new and different kind of culture that could be comfortable with organized violence in the name of the same Jesus. They could go out on expeditions, wars, with flags marked with the sign of the cross and call the wars they waged as 'holy' war or 'just' wars.

But the need for such wars came because now they were no more the community of the poor who had no need to defend their properties; but a community of rich people, officially patronized by the Emperors of Rome.

Over the centuries, the mindset of the Christian communities ceased to be that of the Good Samaritan who would go out and save the broken traveler, risking his own life.

Having detached faith from action, Christians can be liberated from the drudgery of caring for their unfortunate neighbors. Now they became free at last, using this theology of liberation to enjoy a very close relationship with God, just by singing his praise and proclaiming him as Lord.

Liberated form their obligation to love their neighbor as themselves, now they are now free to enslave their neighbors and treat them as slaves.

Christians liberated from the theology of Orthopraxis, using Orthodoxy would be after the people of Africa, not to save them from any misery, but to hunt them in order to enslave them.

Between 1525 and 1866, in the entire history of the slave

trade to the New World, according to the Trans-Atlantic Slave Trade Database, 12.5 million Africans were shipped to the New World. 10.7 million survived the dreaded Middle Passage, disembarking in North America, the Caribbean and South America.[30]

Christians liberated from the teachings of Jesus about identifying themselves with those who are hungry and thirsty would colonize countries after countries, makes its inhabitants their slaves; and missionaries went with these colonizes to 'convert' the enslaved people to Jesus – unmindful of the misery colonization brought to the people they colonized.

Once colonized, a nation suffered diversion of food produced locally to colonizer's homelands, diversion of food crops producing tracts land for production of cash crops, denial of assistance during a crisis, even denying humanitarian assistance during tragedies like the infamous Bengal famine:

The important book "Churchill's Secret War. The British Empire and the ravaging of India during World War II" by Madhusree Mukerjee (Basic Books, New York, 2010) is an account of the forgotten World War 2 Bengali Holocaust, the man-made, 1942-**1945 Bengal Famine in which 6-7 million Indians were deliberately starved to death by the British under Churchill for strategic reasons in what was one of the greatest atrocities in human history but which has been largely white washed from British history**.

Other books have been written about the Bengal Famine Thus N.G. Jog's "Churchill's Blind Spot: India" (New Book Company,

---

30

http://www.theroot.com/articles/history/2014/01/how_many_sl aves_came_to_america_fact_vs_fiction/

Bombay, 1944) in referring to this Bengali Holocaust was the first to **refer to a WW2 atrocity as a "holocaust".** Paul Greenough's "Prosperity and Misery in Modern Bengal: the Famine of 1943-1944" (Oxford University Press, 1982) is a detailed and definitive account of the WW2 Bengal Famine[31]. (Emphasis Added)

But, the British Prime Minister when told of millions dying of hunger would could let them die, diverting the charities of food and medicine sent to hungry people to the already overfed military.

A cursory googling for photographs of 'Bengal famine' would send anyone to sleepless nights, seeing people lying dead on streets, with vultures having their feasts...

The behavior of the Christians who invaded nations makes one wonder if Jesus told these colonizers to go conquer the world with guns and tanks, enslave people – And then as an afterthought called a few to become missionaries, and accompany the colonizers in order to capture 'souls' of himself.

When did ever Jesus lose interest in the body of the poor he served, so that while millions of them died of starvation, he was only interested in the number his missionaries had converted for his church?

All such evils happened because faith that could be only exercised in action got liberated from action, and took refuge in proclamation – a liberation theology spread ever since the Gospel of John came into existence.

---

[31] http://www.countercurrents.org/polya130611.htm

There are more obnoxious things besides colonizing and enslaving of people that the predominantly Christian world was engaged in for centuries. The good pope John Paul II was humble enough to list them out and acknowledge this gross injustice that humanity suffered due to a liberation theology that liberated action from faith. He tendered apologies for over 100 of such wrongdoings, including:

- ➤ The legal process on the Italian scientist and philosopher Galileo Galilei, himself a devout Catholic, around 1633
- ➤ Catholics' involvement with the African slave trade
- ➤ The Church's role in burnings at the stake and the religious wars that followed the Protestant Reformation
- ➤ The injustices committed against women, the violation of women's rights and for the historical denigration of women
- ➤ The inactivity and silence of many Catholics during the Holocaust
- ➤ For the execution of Jan Hus in 1415.
- ➤ For the sins of Catholics throughout the ages for violating "the rights of ethnic groups and peoples, and [for showing] contempt for their cultures and religious traditions".
- ➤ For the actions of the Crusader attack on Constantinople in 1204.
- ➤ On 20 November 2001, from a laptop in the Vatican, Pope John Paul II sent his first e-mail apologizing for the Catholic sex abuse cases, the Church-backed "Stolen Generations" of Aboriginal children in Australia, and to China for the behavior of Catholic missionaries in colonial times.

There is no guarantee that this kind of violence on mass scale has stopped or will stop with the Pope tendering a list of apologies to the world. Because, the Christian world is still living this liberation theology propagated by John's Gospel where one will be judged by their proclamation of faith.

What is needed is the restoration of the spirit of Jesus of Nazareth, the original Spirit of Jesus the Prophet that got lost along the way. For, the world today has millions suffering poverty, hunger, homelessness, statelessness... and Christianity as practiced by dominant countries seems to be a stumbling block to their liberation than a help.

Consider the recent report of how a British Prime Minister and an American President together had invaded Iraq, defying the United Nations, and hiding facts from their people.

From Chilcot Report we learn how they destabilized a whole region by their unjust war on Iraq, on flimsy and false grounds of destroying weapons of mass destruction which they knew did not exist!

They had not only put the lives of their own military personnel at risk, but caused mass destruction to people of Iraq in the name of destroying fictitious weapons of mass destruction.

> Throughout the eight-year occupation (of Iraq by the US and UK forces) and chaotic years since, sectarian war and widespread displacement of communities have ravaged the country. Terror attacks have barely relented, with state-backed militias running riot, and first al-Qaida in Iraq and then Islamic State unleashing murderous savagery.[32]

We could expect Jesus to take the side of the displaced people due to war, and also condemn those who made their lives miserable. And, to be like Jesus, we need to share our lives with and *for* the migrants and stand *against* those who made them

---

32

http://www.theguardian.com/politics/live/2016/jul/06/chilcot-report-live-inquiry-war-iraq migrants and continue to make them so by their arrogance and selfishness.

Helping victims without condemning the victimizers is not a complete act of charity – at, least not in the style and manner of Jesus. With 60 million and more migrants who have nowhere to lay their heads, seeking asylum desperately due to displacement caused by prejudices and wars, the Kingdom of God has not come down to the earth, even after 2000 years since Jesus taught us to pray for and to work for the same.

Jesus And Untouchability

10. WAY FORWARD – JESUS AND HIS UNTOUCHABLES

A. Let's Continue the work of Jesus:
Associate with the downtrodden, Restore their original self-image

It helps to reflect and understand why untouchability is practiced at all.

People who are forced into hard labor all over the world are always treated as low and unworthy of freedom and equal treatment with others in society by some form of untouchability practices only **to strip them of any psychological strength they may have in them to fight back for their rights, and to make them meekly submit to do hard physical labor demanded of them.**

Thus, the common denominator of all practices of discrimination in society is the 'forced labor' the people discriminated against are forced to do, often, in cleaning dirt or in very hard and strenuous physical labor in the fields.

Women at home, not captured from faraway lands, too make for a similar case in traditional societies like in India. The menfolk ensure that the women do all the work at home, and then join them with work in agricultural fields too.

And, men don't help women at home in cooking, washing clothes and utensils, cleaning the home, or to keep their babies clean. Women are made to work more than double of men on any day;

and they get paid less for the same work done in the fields.

Much like homemade slaves, women are taught to feel low about themselves, using their menstruation as a reason.[33] And, they do carry this 'feeling' all through their life, often, even in spite of any amount of their education.

And any work to liberate them starts with healing their injured 'identity' of being "untouchables" (a philosophical identity) or "sinners" (a theological identity) and giving them a new 'identity' of being clean and okay, like everyone else.

To heal their minds and hearts was the challenging task before Jesus. And he was accomplishing this task both by preaching a new message and following a style of life that went against the societal practice of untouchability – by touching them, teaching them.

A touch helps them 'realize they are equal to all human beings, by 'grounding' them from false 'ideas' about themselves; and teaching them helps them clean up the theological mess that they are mired in – a realization that God loves them, and they are not sinners!

And, it is no easy task, as it means aiming and succeeding in redoing deeply held values, beliefs, identities and spirituality of the untouchable people and the rest of the society.

You don't bring into mainstream the people who were

---

[33] For an article on how even the educated behave as if they are impure during menstruation read this article: http://www.youthkiawaaz.com/2016/08/dealing-with-menstrual-taboos/

discriminated against for centuries by just writing in statute books that it is "self-evident" that all "men" are created equal – nor do you convert people who discriminate against them to give up their evil practices by such pious proclamations.

We need to help all men and women 'live' that experience of equality before it will seep into the consciousness of those who discriminate and those discriminated against.

And, Jesus was doing just that by 'associating' with the least in his society.

For instance, we saw how even beggars won't receive alms from tax-collectors. But, Jesus would invite himself to dinner with the tax-collector Zacchaeus telling him "I must stay at your house!" For, his mission compels him to stay with the worst of sinners – to make them feel they are okay with God! It's worth seeing that scene again:

Luke 19: 5-10

[5] And when Jesus came to the place, he looked up and said to him, "Zacchaeus, make haste and come down; for I must stay at your house today." [6] So he made haste and came down, and received him joyfully. [7] And when they saw it they all murmured, "He has gone in to be the guest of a man who is a sinner." [8] And Zacchaeus stood and said to the Lord, "Behold, Lord, the half of my goods I give to the poor; and if I have defrauded any one of anything, I restore it fourfold." [9] And Jesus said to him, "Today salvation has come to this house, since he also is a son of Abraham. [10] For the Son of man came to seek and to save the lost."

The popular 'murmur' reveals the setting in which Jesus proclaims his Good News.

And the conversion Jesus was effecting in Zacchaeus was in

restoring him back to the status of the son of Abraham – an integrated member of Jewish society – from his earlier feeling of being treated as an outcaste. Jesus *chose* to treat this outcaste by including himself in Zacchaeus' house as a *self-invited guest*.

Jesus' behavior that went against the common trend, causing people to murmur, was an integral part of his mission for the untouchables in his society: his touching lepers, dead body of a girl, allowing a women in menstruation to touch him, allowing a sinner-woman to anoint and kiss him, inviting sinners to his house for dinner parties, inviting himself to the house of the worst of sinners as a guest...

Not associating with people other consider as untouchables, we can't affirm their dignity, or join the mission of Jesus.

The world is still full of prejudices of all kinds; and is deeply entrenched in the practice of discrimination, and untouchability even after two thousand years after Jesus.

Two thousand years after Jesus, we still have masses of people we treat as "not-wanted by us in our company" – the migrants, the colored people, the one who does not belong to my religion, my gender, my caste, my country...

Two thousand years after Jesus, we have a Dalit bishop abducted by 'upper caste' priests in Andhra Pradesh in India, stripped, tied, beaten up, trampled upon, and the Church **not rising up in a show of strength to protest the injustice *by associating with those who protest this injustice to the bishop from this downtrodden community.* This not associating shows their acceptance of the caste system**, and their inability to contain the dominance of the dominant castes among its clergy.

We see this folly enacted in gruesome manner, even in this 21st Century the world, proving that the battle to annihilate caste, fighting which Jesus got killed has not been won, yet:

- We do have Dalits in India beaten black and blue for skinning a dead cow, and their getting beaten video graphed and published on the internet! [34]
- A Dalit boy gets murdered in broad day light for having married a non-Dalit girl and the murderers go riding on the crowded street with their blood drenched swords. [35]
- After two thousand years of Jesus, police in the USA killed at least 102 unarmed black people in 2015, nearly twice each week. [36]
- After two thousand years of Jesus, we do have pictures of a baby washed ashore for there was no one – not even among those who claim to follow Jesus – to invite such families to give them protection as they flee for their lives. [37]

We have our deep sense of detest for the poor, the under-privileged, the one not belonging to our race, our religion, our culture, our language, our color, our gender, our sexual orientation... Such sense of detesting and rejecting is

---

[34] A horrible video uploaded by the criminals:
https://www.youtube.com/watch?v=BLgIQYbsNGU

[35] http://www.firstpost.com/india/caste-violence-in-tamil-nadu-dalit-man-murdered-in-full-public-view-for-marrying-upper-caste-girl-2673280.html

[36] http://mappingpoliceviolence.org/unarmed/

[37] http://www.independent.co.uk/news/world/europe/if-these-extraordinarily-powerful-images-of-a-dead-syrian-child-washed-up-on-a-beach-don-t-change-10482757.html

symptomatic of our aloofness and distance from the lives of the poor. It makes a mockery of the life of Jesus, who is venerated for having given up his status as Son of God to be born in a manger, live like a worker, and get killed on the cross with criminals!

We inherit such discriminatory feelings and prejudices, and successfully pass them on from one generation to the next, often, unconsciously; or even wantonly exhibiting their prejudice and flouting all sense of human decency and dignity.

Jesus is a model in shedding our prejudices

Jesus was raised in a highly discriminating society; one that taught its children to discriminate against its own people, and against other races based on the principle and foundation of *Purity and Pollution.*

To appreciate the society he was brought up in, and the degree he could be freed from his prejudices, we may take a look at how even today in Jewish culture women are valued less than men.

In the blog, titled, "Should I Thank God for Not Making Me a Woman?" Rabbi Ari Hart shares with us his anguish related to prayer he recites daily.
"Blessed are you, Lord our God, Ruler of the Universe, who has not made me a woman."
-- Morning Blessings, Artscroll Siddur, p. 12.

"I'm supposed to say that each morning. If I were a woman, I would recite this instead: 'Blessed are you, Lord our God, Ruler of the Universe, who has made me according to Your will.'

"These difficult, even painful blessings are a part of a series of otherwise beautiful meditations thanking God for the everyday gifts of sight, clothes and freedom. Those other blessings roll easily off my tongue, the praise genuine and sincere. But for years I've struggled with praising God for not making me a woman. And I'm not the only Orthodox rabbi who struggles with it.

"As a committed Orthodox Jew, I have accepted the entirety of Halacha -- the Jewish path of law and tradition -- upon myself. This includes guidelines on rituals, holidays, charity, legal matters, sex and, yes, prayers. Not only do I accept it on myself, but as a rabbi, I teach it to others."

It was from such an orthodox religious cultural reality that Jesus had broken himself free from by his association with those considered low. Surely, we can appreciate the role of dad Joseph and mother Mary in instilling in Jesus the meaning of respect for women.

And, we do see Jesus *associate freely* with people whom the elite in his society considered impure. We see him *preach against* the very concept of impurity used to divide people. That's the Jesus Way of affirming the dignity of the people he came down to serve all the way from heaven.

Jesus went to extraordinary length to affirm the dignity people others considered untouchables:

Dignity of life comes from a good self-image. Someone with a shattered self-image is not able to experience the dignity worthy of a child of God.

In one sense, Jesus was at this self-image building work for the broken people, all the time. It was core to his mission on earth. Emmanuel. The sense of GOD WITH US gives his beloved poor people a sense of being on God's side.

We have already seen how much Jesus did to restore dignity to the untouchables by touching the untouchables in his society, and by allowing them to touch him. Now, let's take a closer look at the dinner parties he had with the sinners for the same reason of restoring their lost dignity as children of God.

Besides his working hours, Jesus hosted dinner parties at his home or in some hired places, inviting the untouchables of his society; parties where much time was spent chatting and sharing with guests.

The poor people Jesus invited for dinner must have shared their life of agony, how they got thrown out of traditional livelihood engagements such as farming or animal husbandry, their immediate need for jobs, and misery, in their intimate moments of relationship over meals and drinks with Jesus.

Albert Nolen takes a deep look at this table-fellowship of Jesus with sinners, the poor, the beggars...

> The fact that guests were invited and the fact that they reclined at table show that the meals referred to in the gospels were feasts or dinner parties... Feasts or dinner parties need not be thought of as very elaborate and expensive meals (Lk 10:38-42). The company and conversation mattered more than the food. Nevertheless these dinner parties were such a common feature of Jesus' life that he could be accused of being a drunkard and a

glutton.[38]

And, Nolen argues how the story of Jesus about a king's invited guests excusing themselves could be a reflection of his own predicament of finding his invited dignitaries avoiding him due to his closeness with the untouchables of his society.

Albert Nolen convincingly argues how the *dinners that Jesus had with sinners – by their very nature of breaking the practice of untouchability – would have meant an experience of forgiveness of sins for the poor*. It was an effective restoration of their dignity as beloved children of God.

> It would be impossible to overestimate the impact these meals must have had upon the poor and the sinners. By accepting them as friends and equals Jesus had taken away their shame, humiliation and guilt. By showing them that they mattered to him as people he gave them a sense of dignity and released them from their captivity. The physical contact which he must have had with them when reclining at table (compare Jn 13:25) and which he obviously never dreamed of disallowing (Lk 7:38-39) must have made them feel clean and acceptable.

> Moreover, because Jesus was looked upon as a man of God and a prophet, they would have interpreted his gesture of friendship as God's approval of them. They were now acceptable to God. Their sinfulness, ignorance and uncleanness had been overlooked and were no longer being

---

[38] Albert Nolen, Jesus Before Christianity, Orbis Books, Maryknoll, New York, p. 45

held against them"[39]

For sinners, meals with this man of God broke their sense of feeling unworthy of God. They experienced a deep sense of acceptance by God; A nearness to God; sense of becoming clean and worthy of human touch. For, Jesus has touched them by inviting them for a shared meal and drink.

Udo Schnelle confirms that..."the kind of table fellowship practiced by Jesus constituted an attack on the very foundations of the biblical distinction between 'clean' and 'unclean.'"[40]

Do the downtrodden, unwanted people in society *matter to us* as much as they mattered to Jesus so much that we host parties for them?

Do we do as much as Jesus did, proactively to make the poor, unwanted people feel comfortable, wanted, and secure with material and psychological needs taken care of?

Certainly a lot needs to be and could be done.

B. Let's Read the Bible, Jesus way… Please!
I once went to the house of a friend who has a collection of fancifully printed and bound copies of the Bible. He was happy to show them to me. Looking into them and pointing out to some apparently contradictory passages in the Bible, I asked him how he would choose between them or interpret them. He had a

---

[39] Albert Nolen, Jesus before Christianity, Orbis Books, Maryknoll, New York, 1978, p.48

[40] Robinson, Bob. Jesus and the Religions: Retrieving a Neglected Example for a Multi-cultural World (p. 134). Cascade Books, an Imprint of Wipf and Stock Publishers. Kindle Edition.

ready answer for that. His pastor had told him that the Bible is like a wonderful fish that God has gifted to us. But we must be careful, since this fish comes with bones also, and as bones can get stuck in our throats, we should carefully choose and separate the flesh we love to eat and reject what hurts.

And, *he was asking me repeatedly*, "When there are so many nice passages in the Bible to read, enjoy, ponder about, and benefit from, why would you want to look for problematic passages in the Bible at all! Why don't you just ignore them?"

I had no answer to give him! He was very forthright in what he did with his Bible/s: Choose what is convenient to you and reject what is not pleasing!

Knowingly or unknowingly that's what we have all been doing, all these years. We choose to read only those passages that are supportive of our already held attitudes, values, beliefs, and identities, and we avoid passages that challenge them.

The greatest risk in **choosing what we like** in the Bible comes from the fact that the Bible offers such a wide variety of things to choose from! Choices of positions one incompatible with the other!

Just now we saw such a conflicting position:
Leviticus 16: 2-3
2 The Lord said to Moses...3 Thus shall Aaron come into the holy place: with a young bull for a sin offering and a ram for a burnt offering.

Jeremiah 7: 21-23
21 Thus says the Lord of hosts, the God of Israel: Add your burnt offerings to your sacrifices, and eat the flesh. 22 For in the day that I brought your ancestors out of the land of

Egypt, I did not speak to them or command them concerning burnt offerings and sacrifices. [23] But this command I gave them, "Obey my voice, and I will be your God, and you shall be my people; and walk only in the way that I command you, so that it may be well with you."

If that is the case with the Old Testament – the Bible that Jesus was obliged to follow as a Jew – we have now the addition of the New Testament – which does not in any way reduce contradictory instructions.

Someone who loves equality between genders might quote St Paul and say there is no inequality between male and female among followers of Jesus.

Galatians 3:28

There is neither Jew nor Greek, there is neither slave nor free, there is neither male nor female; for you are all one in Christ Jesus.

But, if you don't believe in gender equality, you may quote the same St Paul from the same New Testament and say:

1 Corinthians 14: 33-35

[33] As in all the churches of the saints, [34] the women should keep silence in the churches. For they are not permitted to speak, but ***should be subordinate***, as even the law says. [35] If there is anything they desire to know, let them ask their husbands at home. For it is shameful for a woman to speak in church. (Emphasis added)

If one loves to keep praying all the time, one may quote:

Ephesians 6:18

Pray at all times in the Spirit, with all prayer and supplication.

Someone not inclined to pray might love to quote the following passage, and argue, if the Father knows what you need before asking, why the hell you pray at all? [After all, if your earthly father does not need your prayers to feed you or clothe you and to take care of your needs, won't God do a better job than your father?]

Matthew 6:7-8

[7]And in praying do not heap up empty phrases as the Gentiles do; for they think that they will be heard for their many words. [8] Do not be like them, for your Father knows what you need before you ask him.

If you loved to hold others slaves, and extract work from them, you have a convenient quote from St Paul in the New Testament. You can even command salves to be obedient to you the slave-master!

Ephesians 6:5-6

[5] Slaves, be obedient to your human masters with fear and trembling, in sincerity of heart, as to Christ, [6] not only when being watched, as currying favor, but as slaves of Christ, doing the will of God from the heart.

But, if you believed in abolition of slavery you'd quote the same New Testament and the same St Paul:

Galatians 3:28

There is neither Jew nor Greek, there is neither slave nor free person, there is not male and female; for you are all one in Christ Jesus.

This passage claims that for the follower of Jesus there can't be any difference between Jews and Greeks (untouchables), male and female, or master and slave. All are equal. There is no discrimination based on race, gender or social status permitted.

Yet, Christians could carry on slave trade or enslave nations as colonies, and for centuries, unmindful of the injunction by Jesus to treat others as you would like them to treat yourself. **It's all a question of how you read the Bible!**

The possibility that we could be quoting the Bible to justify our unethical attitudes, values, and beliefs is very real, and we need, at every step, ensure to read it the way Jesus read his Bible.

Can we just go by what is pleasing to us in the bible, omitting 'bones' that hurt us? Is there a Jesus way of reading the bible? Of choosing the right passages, and making the right interpretations?

The suggestion that we 'choose the right passages' may sound very alarming for traditional Christians who read every word in the Bible as inspired word of God. The real problem is that even the most devout reader 'filters' whatever hurts him/her while reading the Bible. Only they are not aware that they are constantly and consistently filtering passages they don't like, or that makes them feel hurt!

Also it is interesting to note that whatever be the great debate about their understanding of Jesus, all the many warring denominations of Churches *all unanimously omit certain passages* from getting visibility by printing them in their calendars, hanging them on their walls etc. Whatever our denominations, we do agree to ignore or censor the same passages in the gospels.

For instance, any verse that makes the rich uncomfortable such as, "Woe to you who are rich!" won't adorn the wall of any Church or Christian homes, whatever be their denomination. Only thing true about people who believe in reading the bible in its totality is that they are not aware of the omissions they make.

Picking and Choosing Biblical Passages – the Jesus Way!

Jesus had a way of picking and choosing, and interpreting Scriptures.

194

His method was simple. If a passage would not enhanced the life, liberty and human dignity of the oppressed classes, the untouchables in society, the women, the poor, the sinners, the tax collectors of his day **he would daring reject them outright.**

The test of correctness of passages rested on what they did for the least of his little brothers and sisters. In what that passage did for the oppressed classes who are thirsty, hungry, naked, homeless, in prison, sick, and suffered a deep sense of rejection by humans as 'untouchables' by others and rejection by God as 'sinners'.

An example of the way of Jesus

Here is an example of how Jesus deals with a specific provision in the Bible about the right of a husband to divorce his wife by just writing out a bill against her, and putting it her hands.

His Religious leaders forced him to come out in public on his stand on this provision of Biblical Law. Obviously, *his teachings was perceived clearly to be going against this Biblical privilege given to men* and they did expect him to oppose this provision of easy divorce they could avail on flimsy grounds.

And, if Jesus did that, the crowds that hold Bible as their God given Law would be upset, and he could be discredited before them as one going against God.

Mat 19: 3-8

[3] And Pharisees came up to him and tested him by asking, "Is it lawful to divorce one's wife for any cause?" [4] He answered, "Have you not read that he who made them from the beginning made them male and female, [5] and said, 'For this reason a man shall leave his father and mother and be joined to his wife, and the two shall become one flesh'? [6] So they are no longer two but one flesh. What therefore God has joined together, let not man

put asunder." [7] They said to him, "Why then did Moses command one to give a certificate of divorce, and to put her away?" [8] He said to them, "For your hardness of heart Moses allowed you to divorce your wives, but from the beginning it was not so."

Jesus, given his support to women who form half of humanity and who suffer discrimination everywhere in society, wants to say that to divorce a woman on flimsy grounds is certainly wrong. **Jesus does that by appealing to another passage** in the same Bible where it is said that God created humans as male and female, on the last day of his creative activity.

He comments on the law given by Moses saying that the right to divorce was given to them **because they were hard hearted – or uncivilized at the time of Moses.** And he expected them to behave in a more civilized fashion than their ancestors, and told them that they can't take refuge in an archaic Law.

In this incident, Jesus wants them to be guided by a principle of equality between genders **to Judge the Bible itself, and reject a clearly marked instruction that gave a privilege to Jewish men.**

And, Jesus *chooses to quote the **first narrative** of creation* where God created human beings as male and female on **the sixth and last day** of his creative activity. And, he ***interprets it*** to mean that God had intended them to live together, united, right from the beginning.

And, hence, let no man (including Moses) interfere with the arrangement of God!

What makes Jesus choose the (first) story of creation is his choice of "victim's side" in a situation of conflict and unjust male dominance.

Two stories of creation in the Bible

Most often Christians are not aware there are *two stories* of creation in the Bible, and much less that Jesus rejected the second story and chose the first one to claim that Bible taught equality between men and women.

We saw in an earlier chapter how he *ignored the Biblical Laws* that equated menstrual bleeding with impurity, when he told the woman who touched him that she got healed of her illness.

Similarly, in this context of discussion about divorce, too, Jesus ignores the second story, on purpose. In fact, the story of Adam and Eve could help anyone "to defend" divorce.

For, in this second story titled "Another Account of the Creation" in the New Revised Standard Edition, God **first** created Adam from clay on the first day. He gave him the Garden of Eden. Then God proceeded with his creativity activity thus:

Genesis 2: 18-20

[18] Then the Lord God said, "It is not good that the man should be alone; I will make him a helper fit for him." [19] So out of the ground the Lord God formed every beast of the field and every bird of the air, and brought them to the man to see what he would call them; and whatever the man called every living creature, that was its name. [20] The man gave names to all cattle, and to the birds of the air, and to every beast of the field; *but for the man there was not found a helper fit for him.* (Emphasis added)

And, thus, God who created Adam first (on first day?) created Eve at the final phase of creation (on the last day?) *precisely because* **Adam did not find a helper worthy of him in the animals and birds; he was feeling lonely!** This second story that could be used to justify a belief that women are there to entertain men is very popular even today. And, Jesus **carefully avoids referring to this story, because he believed in gender equality, and wanted to defend women from unjust divorce.**

We learn from Jesus that:
- *We need to use scriptures selectively, ensuring we don't perpetuate inequality among humans*
- *We must have clean values **before** entering to read the scriptures.*
- *Right values are those that do good to the untouchables.*

If any scriptural passage goes against the rights and dignity of the weaker sections of society, of those denied their rights, those discriminated against, then:
- We should re-interpret scriptural laws which don't sync with civilized behavior. (E.g. "Eye for an eye" – an example of law of uncivilized people)
- If faced with conflicting versions of Biblical values, *you choose one that spells Good News to the poor, to those denied their right to life, liberty and happiness.*

He reinterprets laws and gives new laws, abandoning old ones:

When Jesus said that Sabbath is for human beings and not for God, *he was giving permission for the poor to work on Sabbath days. For you rest only when you have fed your kids, if not yourself? Failing to feed them, it's okay to work because Sabbath was intended for your welfare by God. God does not get tired, and require rest like us.*

Similarly, Jesus taught that it is not what goes into the body that makes one unclean; but what comes out of the body. Don't we all ensure we eat clean stuff, and not anything stale, contaminated? Obviously food is sacred! But what we produce at the end could be real dirt! That is simple reasoning...

Mark comments that Jesus declared all food clean – implying that in spite of the Bible teaching him to avoid so many different foods, he made *all* food clean. (Mark 7:15)

He *defended his disciples* from feeling guilty when they did what their teachers forbade them to do on Sabbath. For that, he quoted the scriptures to show how David and his men ate the consecrated bread reserved for priests, because they were hungry. (1 Samuel 21:6)

People who are slighted for centuries, who had no hope for their future with any amount of efforts they make, tend to give up and accept their 'fate' as a curse of God. A kind of 'sinner' awareness – one not found worthy of God's favor. Official religion capitalizes on such feeling of inadequacy and unworthiness of the poor.

The religion of Jesus' time made money making poor people feel they are sinners. And, having seen the reality from the side of the poor, living a life of association as a hard manual laborers, he had developed a different understanding of society, religion, and rituals.

Jesus would daringly challenge anything that went to confirm the poor in their sin-consciousness about self. **Jesus did everything first to make them feel clean, and feel wanted and loved by God.**

The religion of Jesus thrived by making the masses feel impure, guilty and sinful, and by teaching about a God and interpreting his words of the Bible in such a way that people believed they were far removed from God, and couldn't hope to be reconciled to him.

Jesus' teaching was in stark contrast with what was being officially taught in his society. Here is a classic example. When Jesus said that it will be as difficult for the rich to enter the kingdom of God as it would be for a camel to enter the eye of a needle, the disciples were astounded. A careful look at their response will tell us a lot about *their belief about God, and who is close to God and who is not*:

That there was so much of 'sin' consciousness among the poor who were suffering due to the Roman oppression is an indicator that the poor being sinners was the ideology propagated by the leaders of Jews among the masses. And, their own personal symbiotic relationships with the Roman rulers was so very obvious. They had the Roman soldiers safeguarding their Temple worship.

While tax broke the backbone of the Jews in the sphere of economy, religion joined hands in fleecing the Jew with so many expenses for purifications of self from one's sins, observation of rituals, festival celebrations, and other acts related to pilgrimages and worships.

If there is one way to please God, to placate Him of one's sins, it was by offering sacrifices to God in the Temple. A costly travel to temple, and costly rituals.

And it naturally followed that only the rich could afford the expenses of religious practices – required to come clean of uncleanness and sins – and hence the popular belief was such that only the rich can be saved.

That the religion as taught by Jesus' religious leaders made it such a burden for the poor to observe can be seen from their response to Jesus in the lines quoted above.

Jesus gave the world a new Image to God

Jesus redefined the very image of God, as a loving Father. He gave them the revolutionary story of God who does not ask for sacrifice to forgive sins, in the story of the prodigal Father. This is indeed reckless Father, prodigal with his love for His children. He is *not happy* with the elder son's unhappiness about his allowing the younger son back into the home and organizing the celebration.

He is (scandalously) more happy with the return of the son whom he had lost than with the one who lived with him faithfully! 'For this son of mine was dead and is alive again; he was lost and is found!' (Lk 15:24). That's like how the one coin you lost and found after much searching makes you more happy than all the coins you have, safe in your pocket, doesn't it?

Jesus taught his people a new way to reach God. Not one based on books and beliefs, but one based on wise reasoning. He taught them how to create a new experience of a loving God, by reasoning: If God cares for birds, His disciples should realize that they are more valuable before God than the birds of the air. (Mat 6:26) If your father cares for you, you can expect the heavenly Father to be much better than him, too.

Luke 11:11
Is there anyone among you who, if your child asks for a fish, will give a snake instead of a fish?

It's like saying you don't have to read the Bible to find facts about your heavenly Father. All you need is to make an assumption that the heavenly Father is a little better than the earthly father. If my earthly father takes care of me so very well, the heavenly Father, I believe, will take even better care of me!

What is 'belief' according to Jesus?

For Jesus, Belief is *not an intellectual activity* of accepting some ideas about God as true as against all other false ideas, with eyes tightly closed, keeping one's facial muscles very tight as a sign of intense belief!

Rather, belief is an attitude one exhibits by one's firm hope that God will certainly act in his/her life, in caring ways, and is shown in one's relaxed demeanor. Look at the birds of the air. They are so very carefree... so should you be, if you believed in God.

Belief, for Jesus is more in the 'letting go' than in 'holding tight'. It is not the 'content' of what you hold that makes your belief great or small... it is the degree of your trust, which invariably exhibits itself in hope of getting out of your predicament.

Even if I were to die the next moment, belief is knowing and relaxing with the firm knowledge that I'll be in the lap of my master the very next moment!

Matthew 6: 25-32

25 "Therefore I tell you, do not worry about your life, what you will eat or what you will drink, or about your body, what you will wear. Is not life more than food, and the body more than clothing? 26 Look at the birds of the air; they neither sow nor reap nor gather into barns, and yet your heavenly Father feeds them. Are you not of more value than they? 27 And can any of you by worrying add a single hour to your span of life? 28 And why do you worry about clothing? Consider the lilies of the field, how they grow; they neither toil nor spin, 29 yet I tell you, even Solomon in all his glory was not clothed like one of these. 30 But if God so clothes the grass of the field, which is alive today and tomorrow is thrown into the oven, will he not much more clothe you— you of little faith? 31 Therefore do not worry, saying, 'What will we eat?' or 'What will we drink?' or 'What will we wear?'

[32] For it is the Gentiles who strive for all these things; and indeed your heavenly Father knows that you need all these things.

Here you see Jesus so beautifully portraying the face of 'belief' so you can touch it, feel it, hear it, smell it and taste it. Faith is living like the birds that chirp and sing the whole day long, least bothered about investments and returns... no toils and hardships to procure things... like the lilies swaying in the breeze... just not worrying even about the most basic things of life...food, clothes, work... **because you believe you are the darling daughter or son of GOD!**

Belief relates to your quality of being...

It's not a philosophical exercise, engaging one in hair-splitting definitions of God and endless theological debates about the nature of God or who the True God is.

Belief is not about God. It is about you.

Belief is not a proclamation. It's a relaxed way of living knowing that God takes care of you! May God lead you through the maze of the written words of God, through the path Jesus took ahead of us!

C. Let's Build Communities that Cooperate, like Jesus did

While he worked and earned his bread, Jesus seems to have spent his money in parties of sharing food and drinks with the poor. His investment was in his relationships with the people.

He started his missionary venture with groups of disciples following him, wherever he went. They were supported by women who were wealthy and who sponsored his mission.

The full force of his teachings on cooperation could be seen only by the way the early followers lived their lives in groups, where they followed the simple philosophy which was adopted verbatim by Karl Marx from the Acts of the Apostles.

We have seen the way early Christians lived a life of total cooperation.

That's the only way the poor can survive and flourish.

More than ever, in a globalized world, we need international cooperation of the poor to learn together, to work together, and share their products and services between them equitably, and make surpluses to provide for harder times.

Cooperation needs these two vital skills:

1. Managerial skill to manage group activity and
2. A deep spirituality that helps to hold the spirit of the people together.

Jesus had experimented it with his team, and his team did establish great cooperatives of Christian communes.

Even today, the Catholic Religious Orders believe in and live as Cooperative Organizations of their own very successfully, and are able to render service to their members and society for hundreds of years, like the Jesuits.

Why not help the poor with so little wealth to pool and manage them in larger productive unites?

Imagine the millions of unemployed youth forming cooperatives that trains them in trades to international standards, and gets them employment all over the world where skilled labor is in short supply?

We may easily make poverty history if we can promote a company of the poor youth in a truly cooperative spirit, like the one a humble parish priest Fr. José María Arizmendiarrieta had established in Spain: The Mondragon Corporation.

Even a cursory look at this corporation will reveal that it succeeded due to the Christian spirit that Fr. José María had instilled in its members: "Now the whole group of those who believed were of one heart and soul, and no one claimed private ownership of any possessions, but everything they owned was held in common."(**Acts 4: 32-35**)

What is needed is to bring back to the youth and the poor workers the spirit of the early Christians where everyone worked in union as a family. Giving their best to the group, and taking care of each one according to their need.

Cooperation to market products/services across globe can help the poor reap the benefit of their labor intensive products and services.

The need for cooperation among the poor is all the more needed when there are multinationals encroaching into their livelihoods such as agriculture or animal farms.

Also, international completion from large scale producers tend to kill miniscule units of production owned by the poor.

There is then an urgent need to protect the poor people's tiny production units from getting drowned under the weight of multinational corporations on price/quality fronts. What else but a cooperative will help them aggregate their production units such as tiny farms or dairies?

And, the spirit of Jesus as demonstrated in the success story of early church communities is the need of the hour to save the poor in the 21st century of a globalized world.

Particularly for the asset deprived poor, the need to gather them, train them as skilled labors and help them reap the benefit of international labor market for skilled workers will be better achieved by their own cooperative, built and supported with the cooperation of international promoters.

Jesus who imaginatively built the most successful of cooperatives particularly for the poorest of the poor of his times must serve us as our inspiration. May his spirit guide us!

D. Let's work for political freedom too, and not accept slavery, like Jesus did

In Moses' time the people of Israel were taken to Egypt and held captives there. But, during the time of Jesus the territory of Israel too was under seizure. It was not only the chosen people but even the promised-land, with Jerusalem its capital, was a colony of Rome.

What they need now was for freedom both for the people, as well as their land. Nothing short of a successful *independence struggle* could achieve that for the Jews. They were looking for a savior from the Roman Empire's colonialism. They even attempted to make Jesus their king. (John 6:15)

But, the escaping of Jesus, avoiding getting crowned a King is no reason to believe that he was *for continued slavery of Jews under the Romans*! Or that he was not interested in taking sides with the masses who aspired for liberation.

After escaping from taking up the role of a king, Jesus did not go about preaching, "Let us pay our tax to Caesar since God has given him as our ruler; and to the temple all that the priests demand of you! God bless our King! Long live Caesar!"

If his teachings were in those lines, certainly, people longing for freedom *could not have thought of* making Jesus their King. Their very desire to crown him king is an expression of not only their political ambitions, but also their faith in Jesus as the right leader for their political freedom: replacing the monarch in Rome with their own Jewish King: Jesus!

Had Jesus taught them to remain humble slaves all through, then there was no Good News left in Jesus' teachings to his untouchable followers.

For, the root of untouchability lay in their poverty caused by the greedy Romans colonizers who taxed them endlessly.

In fact Jesus' leanings and support for the aspirations for independence of his people must have been well known. Otherwise, there is no meaning in the *"trap"* laid to capture him by making him come public with his statement on paying tax to Caesar.

If Jesus was preaching to the people to pay tax to Caesar faithfully, where then is the trap laid to catch him on the question of paying tax?

Note the question. "Is it *lawful* to pay taxes to Caesar or not!" Doesn't it sound weird to ask someone "Do you think it is lawful to pay your taxes to your Government?" Laws are to be obeyed. Tax laws are no exceptions. You don't have to go to Jesus to clarify your doubt if you should obey tax laws. (It is enough if you defaulted paying your taxes; you'll be taught by force if the laws are to be obeyed or not!) The Law referred to are Mosaic Law, the laws of the Bible. It implies, "Can you be a good Jew and still pay tax?"

Taxes belong legitimately to the Government in a democracy, and to the King or Queen in a monarchy. Had democracy been present there would be nothing profound in the statement of Jesus if he had said "Pay your taxes to the Government" in such a context.

But Jesus was in a nation under subjugation. To say you continue to pay taxes was tantamount to saying you should continue to be in slavery! That's not a very good news for those languishing in slavery! Such a message can *only* be Good News for the illegitimate colonizers.

Jesus' answer is not about paying taxes at all. He asked for a coin to be shown to him:

> "This coin had the effigy of the emperor and the superscription on one side: Emperor Tiberias Son of Divine Augustus." On the reverse side, some coins had a female figure facing right...[41]

This was an insult to Jews who had fought against Pilot bringing and installing the bust of Caesar in Jerusalem – to carry the same image in their pockets. (See the next quote)

"He said to then, "Well then, give back to Caesar the things that belong to Caesar and to God the things that belong to God" The (Greek) verb ("apodeste") is best translated "give back" rather

---

[41] David E Garland Exegetical Commentary on the New Testament – Luke; Harper Collins

than simple "render" or "give".[42]

Jesus in effect asks Jews to declare Roman currency counterfeit in Israel. Not to have the coins at all because they bear Caesar's image.

They 'marveled' his answer because he escaped their trap. They could not make him an enemy of the Government for he was asking them to pay more than the tax! The currency is of Caesar, and pay him what 'belongs' to him.

People of Israel, to this day, detest having 'images' for God or humans in their land. There should be no statue for anyone. Their coins, even today, don't bear the image of anyone, unlike the coins/notes of other nations.

And, Pilate the Governor of the Jews wanted to bring in the images of the Emperor of Rome into Israel, and this is the lesson he learned:

> Pilate is no friend of the Jews. One of his first official acts is to order Roman troops in Jerusalem to decorate standards with busts of Emperor Tiberius. When the people rise up in protest of these graven images, which are forbidden by Jewish law, Pilate responds by having his soldiers surround the protesters and draw their swords as if to attack. The Jews refuse to back down. Instead, they bend forth and extend their necks, making it clear that they are prepared to die for their beliefs. For the first time, Pilate sees with his own eyes the power of the Jewish faith.[43]

---

[42] ibid

[43] Bill O'Reilly; Martin Dugard. Killing Jesus: A History (Kindle

When asked about tax, Jesus *cleverly diverts the debate* on to their carrying graven images in their pockets! If all the Jews of the land had earlier joined as one individual to protest with a determination to die for their belief about not allowing graven images into Israel, Jesus wanted to know how they were carrying the same graven images of Caesar in their pockets!

He cleverly diverted the debate by asking anyone to show him a coin. And, asked the question, whose mage is this! It was as good as telling them, "How shamelessly you are carrying Caesar's image in your pockets after sending back his images earlier. Now, these coins *belong to* Caesar because the image on it belongs to him. Give the coins back to him! Not just pay taxes. But return *all his* coins as they have his *images*. It is sinful to carry or have them in Israel."

[You have a photo in your hand and someone asked you whose photo it is. If you said it is the photo "of my" classmate, you are saying in effect it is **not** mine! Next the question would be why do you keep it? And not return to the owner.

Ownership and image get linked in a mysterious way!

Jesus cleverly plays on the word "whose image" and the answer the image "belongs to Caesar"]

How wonderful was Jesus' answer! While he was not denying that they should pay taxes, he was reminding the Jews of the urgency to get free of Roman Rule, by rejecting the currency of Rome! And, they should reject the currency (equal to the rule of

---

Locations 1016-1021). Macmillan. Kindle Edition.

Rome) as vehemently as they did when Pilate tried to bring in graven images of Caesar did!

But, unfortunately, we have heard time and again that Jesus was preaching colonized people to pay tax to colonizers.

Preaching good news to untouchable poor definitely puts Jesus in conflict with those who made them poor and who benefit by keeping them poor. In fact the test of dedication to the untouchables is in the protest it raises from those who consider themselves pure and avoid the untouchables.

As noted earlier in this book, Jesus did go underground, living under the protection of the people considered untouchable by Jews. And we know that he was ready to give his life for the social-religious stands he took – even to the death on the cross.

John 11: 53-54

[53] So from that day on they took counsel how to put him to death.[54]Jesus therefore no longer went about openly among the Jews, but went from there to the country near the wilderness, to a town called Ephraim; and there he stayed with the disciples.

Had Jesus restricted his ministry to serving their poor with only healing the sick or raising the dead, and teaching people with wonderful stories, he would have been a celebrity among his Jewish people and remained so to this day.

But, his work was not just works of "charity" to the poor, but one that sought to remove the cause of their poverty: both the religious and political causes of their slavery and misery.

D.   Let us unite in faith across religions – even as like Jesus did

Jesus who all along believed in the superiority of the Jewish race was floored. He not only acknowledged that non-Jews will enter God's kingdom, but also that people (uncircumcised people?) from east and west – that is from all world religions – will come and partake of God's heavenly eternal feast.

Jesus' declaration that religion is no bar to reach heaven that was captured by the evangelists has not been appreciated yet by Christians. Jesus was a Jew. He died a Jew. And, he believed first that only Jews were entitled to heaven after death, to the exclusion of all other races.

But, Jesus had changed his belief after seeing a non-Jew's faith that was much greater than what he saw among his own countrymen.

This openness of Jesus is the need of the hour, if the world should get over the religion based prejudices being whipped up by selfish people everywhere for their ugly political gains.

May the spirit of Jesus guide us across religious barriers to build cooperatives of all those who believe in love – particularly love for people the world rejects, considers impure, or unworthy of their association – the untouchables Jesus was fond of associating with

EPILOGUE

In my training classes, I ask trainees to keep a pen and paper ready to do an exercise. And, I tell them to draw what they understand by the word "chair" in 30 seconds. And, write two to three words that describe what their chairs are made of: Iron, plastic, leather, wood etc.

And, if there are fifty people in the room, you may have fifty different images and descriptions of what a chair is. Yet we think we are speaking of the same thing while we are talking of a chair when in fact we may think of different things.

And, so with any word. Be it a pen or even God! Some think of God as a Male. Some as Female. A Saivaite saint poet Maniakka Vachakar would think of his God as Male-Female & Neither.

Does Bible always talk of God as a male God? May be not: aren't there reference to God protecting you like a hen protecting its chicks inside her wings? If so what is the gender of God?

The council of Nicaea was called by an emperor and they were able to decide on the nature of God, and those who did not fall in line with the definitions were condemned as 'heretic' and their writings were banned...

This kind of 'certainty' about Cristian's knowledge of God the 'true' God became the obsession of Christians for too long.

St Ignatius of Loyola, for instance, was arrested thrice by the 'inquisition' and tried because he was preaching about Jesus without a degree in theology! God for us has become an 'object' of study and could be mastered with a university degree!

Ancient religion born in India knew better. The sages and sacred books here advocate a search into not the nature of God, but of humanity. Is it ever possible to know who you are? You are not your body. Yet, we identify ourselves with our body.

We are not even our minds. Our thoughts are what we create. We create a thought that makes us happy; next moment we can create a thought that makes us angry, or sad... The question is who is it that is producing this thought? Who am I who is behind these thoughts?

But how easily we say, "**I'm** happy. **I'm** angry or **I'm** sad?

Unfortunately, Christianity got caught up in a world of ideas that we generate, without trying to understand who we are.

Jesus became a public figure after he had the experience of "I am the beloved son of God" during baptism. That was not a thought. But an experience that transformed him from a mason or carpenter that he was, to a rabbi. People who have such transformative experience that are called 'awakening' don't go about preaching "Look here! I'm an awakened master. Come and worship me." One effect true awakening has on people is that they become passionate about helping others to wake up! You too are a beloved daughter of God. Son of God. Child of God.

The awakened Buddha went about on a mission to awaken everyone to their own Buddha nature. Not to make himself an object of worship by all.

Every enlightened sage in India did the same. Once they had

realized their true nature as more than what meets the eye, that they are in a deep way a manifestation of the ultimate reality called God, they went about inviting others to their own deeper awakening. Often such things happen in silence; when you go beyond the world of words and ideas; when you succeed in silencing your mind that refuses to quieten.

Jesus was there alone for forty days after he had a self-realization-experience on the banks of Jordan that he was indeed God. That experience has more to do with silence than words and preaching. That was an 'experience' that can't get transmitted in words; that was an experience of a lightning and thunder and the opening of heaven.

An experience that can't be replaced by the splendor of an emperor walking amidst fighting bishops dressed in purple and gold or dazzling diamonds and settling who among the hundreds of bishops knows the exact nature of God in the form of written and spoken words!

Words distract. God certainly is not a thing that can be defined rightly. Any definition of God is proof that what you have defined is NOT God. For God can't be held in a definition.

By definition infinity is what defies definition. Once defined it can't be infinity. But we know God is such and such. "He" has six characteristics! Any one contradicting is not knowing God, and is a heretic to be burned alive!

That's why a great sage like Ramana Maharishi would confirm a Tamil saying "Those who saw God don't speak, and those who speak haven't seen God!" In one sense, trying to capture God in words is heresy number one. But, we have people who preach God as if they have God in their pockets; and they distribute

God... the true God, all in the name of Jesus!

Jesus had to be requested by his disciples to teach them to pray! Then he taught them the brief prayer. His teachings on God were embedded in stories. For, we can only tell stories about God. God can't be captured in neat definitions of philosophy or theology. "He" is 'like' a father who forgives. To understand that see what your dad does. He does not give you a piece of stone if you asked for bread? Be sure, the heavenly Father is a better father than yours. If He will care for the birds of the air, let us believe He cares for us.

The exercise in Nicaea taken up by the bishops was wordy. They tried to capture God in words.

It took them away from the Jesus experience the early disciples had with Jesus. The experience of an awakened Jesus during his life time. And, the experience of an arisen Jesus after he was taken away from our midst.

Basically it is an experience. A deeply transforming experience. An experience that converts people from their selfishness to transcendence. To give up their properties, and give to the community. To the poor.

It was decided at Nicaea that those who held Jesus to be the same as God and those who taught different things were condemned and eliminated from the scene.

That such an effort to get at the right definition proved futile as is witnessed by the number of 'churches' that have come up with believers in the same Jesus, holding the same bible in hand.

It is futile to go after a definition of God. Hinduism is wise. It teaches you to find who you are first.

You are under an illusion. Illusion that you know things, that you can know even God! But, get out of that illusion by discovering who you really are.

Jesus realized he was God. He calls us to have that same realization. He assures us that God's kingdom is within you, buried deep.

But, we have very little tools to explore beyond the illusory awareness of me being my body or me being my thought.

That's what yoga is all about. Leading you to gradually still your mind, and realize your true self. That's how the great sage Patanjali defines yoga: "Yoga is absolute quietening of the wavering mind."

Getting beyond words that keep rising as thoughts, in the ultimate silence, we can realize "I am God." In India we call this awakening, enlightenment, or God-Awareness. Awareness that I am God! I'm Shiva. I'm Brahma.

Jesus knew he was God. And once he knew that he started his ministry of service, helping people realize their own Godhood. For we are the true images of GOD. Not untouchable sinners. That was Jesus' mission: No untouchables but Gods... Hence, when you serve the untouchables, you serve Jesus, you serve true God...

Let's conclude with this story:

> A Jesuit priest went to Japan to study in a Zen monastery. He said that after sitting in meditation for long hours his legs would often begin to ache terribly. The master advised him on proper procedure and then asked what practice he was following in meditation. The Jesuit explained that he was

sitting silently in the presence of God without words or thoughts or images or ideas. The master then asked if his God was everywhere. The Jesuit nodded his head, "yes." He asked if he was wrapped around in God, and the answer again was yes.

"Very good, very good," said the master. "Continue this way. Just keep on. And eventually you will find that God will disappear and only you will remain." The Jesuit was offended by this for it sounded like a denial of his sacred beliefs. He contradicted the master and said, "God will not disappear. But I might disappear and only God will be left." "Yes, yes," the master agreed, smiling. "It's the same thing. That is what I mean."

- Dick Sutphen in "The Oracle Within"

ABOUT THE AUTHOR

Arulraja, 63, is teaching Business Ethics and Human Resource Management in a Jesuit run St. Joseph's Institute of Management in Bangalore, India, from 2015. He holds a degree in Law, MA in Economics, an MBA and MPhil in Entrepreneurship.

Between 1970 and 1991, he was a Jesuit, working in the province of Andhra Pradesh. When he left the Order, he was heading the Jesuit University Youth Ministry for the State of Andhra Pradesh (AICUF), and was the Social Action Coordinator for the Jesuit Province of that State.

Most of his life has been spent in studying and working for the liberation of the people still considered and treated as untouchables, mostly through his training programs and writings.

The International Labor Organization gave him consultancy to author a Training Manual for use among rural women in Thrift-Credit Self-Help Groups. ILO published it under title "From Poverty to Prosperity".

His other published books are "Jesus the Dalit" and "Achieving Rural Development Using Neuro-Linguistic Programming" (https://www.amazon.com/Achieving-Rural-Development-Neuro-Linguistic-Programming/dp/8190258303)

He continues his mission among Dalits, the untouchables of India, with a vision to promote their development in the social and economic spheres of life, through training aimed at building self-help and Cooperation.

Jesus And Untouchability

www.ingramcontent.com/pod-product-compliance
Lightning Source LLC
LaVergne TN
LVHW051506080426
835509LV00017B/1939